Happy Birthday
Sid

Love

Magnolia
Blossom

MAYFLOWER
MANNERS

MAYFLOWER MANNERS

Etiquette for Consenting Adults

by

SYDNEY BIDDLE BARROWS

and

ELLIS WEINER

DOUBLEDAY

New York London Toronto Sydney Auckland

PUBLISHED BY DOUBLEDAY

a division of Bantam Doubleday Dell Publishing Group, Inc.
666 Fifth Avenue, New York, New York 10103

DOUBLEDAY and the portrayal of an anchor with a dolphin
are trademarks of Doubleday, a division of
Bantam Doubleday Dell Publishing Group, Inc.

Library of Congress Cataloging-in-Publication Data

Barrows, Sydney Biddle.
Mayflower manners : etiquette for consenting adults /
by Sydney Biddle Barrows and Ellis Weiner. — 1st ed.
        p.   cm.
1. Etiquette.   2. Sexual ethics.
I. Weiner, Ellis.   II. Title.
BJ1854.B37   1990
395—dc20   89-23385
        CIP
ISBN 0-385-26245-0

To Bobby
for being The Best

CONTENTS

𝓘NTRODUCTION

𝓐ssuming it not inappropriate to couple so rude a word as "boom" with the fine and elegant "etiquette," then we may say that over the last ten years or so, there has been in America something of an etiquette boom. Many books have been published explaining not only classic matters of deportment, courtesy, table manners, etc., but more up-to-date issues as well, such as second weddings performed by female rabbis, how to eat a kiwi, and how to write a thank-you note to a college roommate who has become one's stepmother.

Such works are useful, and provide much valuable information. But they never go far enough. Either they omit mention of subjects deemed (by them) to be inappropriate for a discussion of etiquette, such as sex, or they simply fall behind the times. One common complaint about most books of etiquette is what could be called their exhaustive incompleteness: the standard etiquette book is as big as a brick, weighs only a little less, and still cannot tell us how to behave in situations in which our anxiety far outstrips what we feel when confronted with an oyster fork at a formal banquet.

Thus the need for *Mayflower Manners*.

By this title we do not mean etiquette as practiced by the Pilgrims in the seventeenth century. We mean, rather, an approach to the etiquette of daily life in which as much attention is given to the informal, private ways in which men and women interact as to the formal and public ways. Hence the allusion of the title to the background of one of the authors, whose familiarity with the private goings-on of the sexes—particularly as they contrast with their publicly professed beliefs—is well known.

Now, one "real" way in which men and women interact is by having dinner, granted. But another is by going to bed. Some have said that what goes on in private between two adults is not subject to the dictates (or, rather, the cheerily helpful suggestions) of etiquette. But, as is explored in a bit more detail in the pages that follow, we submit that good manners are, if anything, even more important in the bedroom than in the dining room. Where else are one's innermost feelings so exposed, so subject to injury, so, as it were, naked? If it is etiquette's business to minimize bad feeling among people (N.B.: to minimize; not to eliminate completely), then it is high time it set up shop where men and women really do want, as we say elsewhere, "to do the right thing."

We say "men and women" because a central theme of *Mayflower Manners* is precisely the ways in which relations between the sexes have changed over the past, say, thirty years. The list of influences that have shaped interactions of the sexes since World War II is familiar but striking: modern feminism beginning in the 1950s; the reawakened interest in social justice with the civil rights movement in the late fifties and early 1960s; the emphasis on personal choice, pleasure, and "participatory democracy" in the 1960s; the women's liberation movement and the advent of both "lifestyle" and "self-realization" in the 1970s; the mass migration of women into all levels of the work force in the 1980s.

There has also been a series of reactions and retrenchments: from the sexual liberality as fostered by The Pill to the "safe sex" caution inspired by the proliferation of sexually transmitted diseases; from the Sisterhood Is Powerful solidarity of many educated young women of one generation to the I'm-no-feminist qualifications of their younger sisters; from the All You Need Is Love attitude of the sixties to the Greed Is Good credo of the eighties.

Such spectacular social change has generated a pervasive and tenacious uncertainty about many aspects of daily life, one which often concerns issues that deal not so much with etiquette as with ethics. The distinction is important, but we will at times play fast and loose with it. "Etiquette," as used in these pages, refers to formal interactions between individuals, as codified by convention. "Ethics," on the other hand, refers to the underlying values of a particular system. It is unethical to steal an idea from your colleague and pass it off as yours; it is bad manners to sneeze on him while doing so. Call ethics the domain of mortal sin, of the felony, while etiquette concerns the venial, the misdemeanor.

In what follows, we will be tempted to stray off the tidy green lane of etiquette onto the roaring paved road of ethics. We will announce this, and apologize for it, and discuss its implications, when it happens. And it will happen, since in *Mayflower Manners* we aim to discuss issues that have been overlooked by the usual etiquette arbiters—issues which are born of new movements and trends in society, which start out as ethical or legal, and only after implementation give rise to the assumed rules of appropriate behavior we call good manners.

We have derived our opinions and rulings from various sources, chief among which are people "in the field"— i.e., individuals with differing kinds of expertise, either socially or professionally, with whom we have discussed problems specific to their areas of knowledge. Throughout, we have tried to be consistent: to favor discretion over self-assertion, respect for the other person over selfishness, giving a little over having it all.

Where an expert confessed he or she had no definitive ruling about a matter, we asked what was commonly done or believed. Therefore what follows is at least in part an educated guess about what's right, rather than a final ruling from on high. All such respondents, expert or amateur, are referred to as "sources." The result is, if anything, the opposite of an objective scientific discussion of our subject. No attempt has been made to cull a representative sampling or derive a definitive cross section of anything. This is not sociology.

On the contrary, this is fun. We have sought to balance usefulness of information with readability of style. We hope the lightness of the tone does not undermine the seriousness of the information or opinions it is used to express. Etiquette isn't exactly a day at the beach of self-indulgence, but it needn't be a lifetime in the salt mines of "propriety."

Finally, we'd like to thank those men and women who shared their time and thoughts with us, without whom this work would have been impossible.

Sydney Biddle Barrows
Ellis Weiner
July 1989

Sydney Biddle Barrows wishes to extend her thanks, appreciation, and warmest thoughts to all of the following, some just for being such wonderful friends, some for their help in writing this book, and some for both!

Michael Abandond
Wabel Abdallah
Mr. & Mrs. William Allen
Norma Jean Almodovar
Jim Black
Allan Block
Dallas Boesendahl
Beth Bontley
Nancy Bonwit
Nissan Boury
Paul Bresnick
Ed Callaghan
Richard Currier
Daphne Davis
Mark Denbeaux
Risa Dickstein
Vic Donohue
Maddy & Marty Dubin
Catherine Edelman
Andrea Farber
Dianne Feeney
Linda Feldman
Linda & Justin Feldman
Gigi & Chick Fisdell
DiAnne Fishel
Sheri Frahm

Montgomery Frazier
Jacqueline & Stanton
    Freeman
Tom Gates
Pat Grantham
Anthony Herrera
Rick Higgins
Beauregard Houston-
    Montgomery
Michael Katz
Doris & Irving Liebman
Patrick McMullen
Jonathan Marder
Jeff Martin
Dr. Hugh Melnick
Jim Piazza
Melinda Pike
Robert Posey
Jane & David Quinn
Matthew Rich
Jimmy Roe
Audrey Smaltz
Colby Smith
Sydney Smith
Leigh Stewart
Dale Stine

Ann Watt Marianne Strong
Ellis Weiner Topsy Taylor
Jim Tracy
Ken Warner
Richard Weisman
Larry West
Chris Westwood
Ed Williams
Andrea Wohl

Ellis Weiner's appreciation goes to:

Jan Bowers
Paul Bresnick
Peter Ginsberg
Alfred Glossbrenner
Bruce Yaffe
Steven Zipperstein

MAYFLOWER MANNERS

IN
PUBLIC

INTRODUCTIONS

In General: The idea of "the etiquette of introductions" is in some ways a redundancy. The mere act of introducing someone, or yourself, to someone else, regardless of how crudely, is by its very nature an act in observance of etiquette. (The act of introducing yourself to yourself has less to do with etiquette than with abnormal psychology.) There may be an aspect of human life involving two people in which etiquette does not, or at least may not, play a part. But it is hard to think of what it might be, short of the two people attempting to kill one another without exchanging a cordial greeting. There may even be an etiquette for mutual homicide, but it is not part of *Mayflower Manners*.

Having said that, it remains to be added that there are right ways and wrong ways of introducing oneself and others. The basic rules are firmly established: Introduce an inferior to a superior, a man to a woman, a younger person to an older person, a child to an adult, a dog to a human. One way to introduce yourself is to extend your hand for a handshake and say, "How do you do? I'm John Smith." If the other person asks, "How do I do what?" he is being rude. On the other hand, so are you, since your name is probably not really John Smith. You may thus proceed with your interaction. Out of such exchanges comes civilization itself.

A FACE IN THE CROWD

Introducing another to a group of people is difficult enough—no one is quite sure how many names must be announced—and introducing yourself to a group is even worse. But what if you add to that context an ulterior motive, i.e., flirting? What if your design in introducing yourself has from the start been to gain the attention of one person from among the crowd? Is there a way to signal that, **to selectively introduce yourself to one person among many**?

In fact there is, depending on the nature of the gathering. If you are the guest of honor, the featured speaker, the birthday boy or girl, then you have a public role to fulfill and may not play favorites until the general introductions are out of the way and the group has broken up into smaller tête-à-têtes.

But if your role in the group is that of merely another socializer, you may drift up as the group enjoys its conversation, gravitate toward the person in whom you are interested, make arbitrary-seeming comments to that person about the topic at hand, and at a suitable break, using that rudimentary contact as your excuse, introduce yourself to him or her. The group is a nation, your introduction your passport. So long as you show it at the border, what does it matter which port of entry you select?

This strategy has a dual effectiveness: Not only are you able to focus on the individual you prefer, but by thus throwing yourself at his or her mercy as a stranger in need of assistance, you force the other person to learn your own name as he or she introduces you to the others.

And if he or she is not any more a part of the group than you, the two of you have that much more in common, and you can propose separating from the rest.

It all sounds rather suave, doesn't it? And it always works—at least, it does in 1930s romance movies and screwball comedies, where everyone's manners are impeccable and people are destined to meet because it's written, if not on the pages of Fate, then on the pages of the script. In real life, outcomes differ. Your quarry might smile vacantly and then ignore you, making you feel rejected and foolish. You might counter with "You're not being very polite, you know." But don't. That's rude.

But now you are the other person. This individual, who seems to fancy himself a character in a 1930s romance movie or screwball comedy, has selected you as his chaperone or sponsor or confidant. It takes only a casual hand gesture to show him you are married, but if you are not? How to tell him you are in love with another, or on a date with another, or simply **not interested**?

You can't, but you needn't, and besides, you shouldn't. At least, not so soon. Flirting comes in a wide range of styles, from the imperceptibly subtle to the off-puttingly obvious. But its ultimate goal can never be assumed. To snub someone whose introduction you think implies romantic interest, before he/she has had a chance to declare (well, hint at) his/her intentions, is enormously presumptuous, not a little conceited, and fantastically impolite.

Introducing yourself as a means of singling someone out of a group may be a precondition of serious flirting, but it does not necessarily imply that that is what is going on. The person may simply want to talk to you. Indeed, times being what they are, the person may simply want to flirt with you, intending it to go no further than that.

YOUR MUTUAL FRIEND

Isn't it nice when someone we know introduces us to someone we might like? Isn't it not so nice when someone we know **introduces us to someone we're *commanded* to like**?

Such introductions are usually made with the best of intentions but the worst of techniques: "Helen," says Hilary. "This is Howard. Howard's just getting over a divorce, so he's ripe for picking, Hel." Or, "Jill," James says, "This is Jack. You two are perfect for each other." The result of such an introduction is invariably some nervous, forced laughter, a few blurted non sequiturs, and a small etiquette vacuum left in the wake of the merrily departing introducer. Jack and Jill or Howard and Helen are left looking at each other and wondering, if only for a second, what to say now that their friend has gotten things off on the wrong foot.

Naturally, one thinks of something: "Oh that Hilary," one of them says. "What a card." Or, to the chucklingly oblivious James, Jack might say, "We'll be the judge of that." If no witty rejoinder comes to mind, one simply ignores the gaffe and carries on as though everything has been perfectly discreet.

Note that in manners terms this is not a capital crime, nor is there usually anything malevolent in such behavior. It could even be argued that it provides the two people being introduced a common subject to start discussing. But when the ice has to be broken, it's better to use a chisel or a pick than a sledgehammer. Professional or amateur matchmakers, busybodies, and yentas should be aware that regardless of how lightheartedly such "helpful" introductions are made, they are impolite. Even in the latter case above, in which no real personal details are revealed, the two strangers (which is what, by definition, they are) are stuck with a third party's agenda, which they must take pains either to neutralize or ignore. Howard's divorce, in the first case, may be front-page news, but a joshingly casual mention of it, or similar personal matters, within the tightly circumscribed public ritual of an introduction, is the height of vulgarity.

A POPULAR MSCONCEPTION

But now suppose that Helen and Howard, having been properly introduced, address one another in a formal but not untitillating manner, using each other's surnames. She calls him "Mr. Coward," he calls her "**Ms.** Melon." Yes, "mzz." Why not? True, "Ms." looks like a strictly orthographic convenience that should never be pronounced, like "Ph.D." But it is an appropriate and courteous substitute for "Miss," to be used in conversation as well as in correspondence. If one happens to know that the lady in question dislikes "Ms." and prefers "Miss," then she may be introduced and addressed as such. But when in doubt use "Ms.," the whole point of which is to accord respect to a lady regardless of whether or not she is married.

What if, aside from not being married, she is not completely out of puberty? How to know **when to address a girl as "Miss," or "Ms."**? The answer is obvious: Use "Miss" for as long as the young lady is a girl, i.e., too young to be married even if she wants to be. If you guess wrong—if the fifteen-year-old you have called "Miss" snaps, "It's Mrs.!"—your embarrassment will be overwhelmed by your amazement, and no one, except the married child in question (to whom you may apologize), will blame you.

And if **the lady herself objects to its use**? May she correct the presenter and those she is meeting? There is nothing wrong, when shaking hands, with a friendly, "I prefer Miss Melon, actually." It might mark you as a traditionalist, a fact which you may or may not wish to exploit. It will also afford you a chance to pronounce your name once more, helping the person you've just met (whose name you don't remember) to remember it. Of course, the opposite ploy can be used to great effect, too: introduced as "Miss," you shake the other's hand, smile, and say, "Actually, I prefer Ms. Melon."

This all-purpose qualification can also be useful when your host has mispronounced your name.

PUT IT THERE

As for **the handshake**: The rule used to be that men waited for women to offer their hands. Today, however, anyone may make the first move. And while it would seem a self-evident bit of child's play to shake hands properly, the fact is that many women, and even men, don't do it right. For them, then, this brief but impassioned primer.

Amazingly, there are still men whose handshake is so weak, tepid, and blood-chilling, it inspires flights of horrified poetry in others seeking to describe it. **A weak handshake**—and we speak here of men shaking hands with men, of course; a lady is by definition never "weak"—is, when conveyed by even the driest hand, a clammy, dispiriting thing. You reach out in virile expectation of a solid grip and a firm fistful of sinew; you get, instead, the back of a raw chicken. You are waiting for the other fellow's grasp to send a taut ripple of manly energy into your hand and up your arm. You get, instead, the fluttering bone and flaccid skin of a dying bat, which draws out your own vigor in a spiteful, last-ditch vampire effort to sap your natural vitality. Men object to a weak handshake, not because it is "effeminate," but because it is moribund, antilife, a concession of defeat and exhaustion before things have even begun. And its effect lingers, often for years: for some reason, one remembers the experience, perhaps because it is so hard to believe that the bad handshaker is not aware of what he is doing and its effect.

Having thus unburdened ourselves of this prejudice, we might still wonder: Is a febrile, limp, lily-livered handshake impolite? Not technically; the only outright form of insult with regard to hand shaking is to decline (i.e., ignore) the offer altogether. But it can be infuriating nonetheless. Those so angered, having recovered from the momentary nausea and despair engendered by a bad handshake, should take care not to destroy the other's hand in fury. The proper response to a weak handshake is a good handshake, not a lethal one. In this, as in all of etiquette, the appropriate response to bad manners is a display of exemplary manners, in the covert hope of either educating or embarrassing the other.

Which brings us to **the bone crusher, the hand pulverizer**. It will not have escaped the reader's notice that

some men in modern society can be maniacally competitive. This tendency extends, literally, to their handshakes; every encounter, for such individuals, offers an
opportunity to blast the opponent (i.e., any other man)
with a charge of muscle and confidence in order to claim
the advantage and see what the other guy is made of, or
what he used to be made of before he lost the use of his
now-demolished right hand. The technique is simple:
Take the other gentleman's hand in yours and go through
it like a nutcracker through a walnut, without mercy or
hesitation. It takes a degree of brute strength to do this,
and a degree of brute brutishness to take pleasure in the
pain it causes. However, this, too, is less a matter of
etiquette than of something else—paleoanthropology,
perhaps. Experts in the rituals of cavemen and cave-
women, cave society and cave handshakes, should be
consulted for further information.

As for the good handshake, it can be a thing of beauty,
an exchange of life-force in a socially acceptable manner.
The other's hand, be it female or male, is grasped firmly
but not psychotically, and then shaken once or twice.
Not squeezed, like a lemon over a cup of tea, not pal-
pated lightly like a breast in a doctor's examination room;
not held and immediately released, like a failed effort
to save someone from drowning, not worked for minutes
like a barnyard pump. The correct force lies somewhere
to the weak side of what it takes to open a set of jumper
cables and to the strong side of what it takes to break a
loaf of French bread in half. The proper shake is a smart
one-two.

A handshake is always in order, whether among colleagues, friends, or newly introduced strangers. Are there

times **when it is inappropriate**? Only the obvious ones: when one of the greeters is handicapped, when the hands are irredeemably dirty, when one's arms are full of packages, when infirmities (arthritis, e.g.) prevent one from responding. If the latter is the case, it can be mentioned by way of brief apology.

Finally, there is the square-dance-like spectacle of **groups of people all shaking hands with one another**. (A common example of this can be seen at the start of pro football games, particularly any year's Super Bowl, where a bevy of "team captains" meet and greet at midfield before the coin toss.) It requires a Broadway choreographer and a mainframe computer to direct smoothly the shaking of multiple hands by multiple hands; for this reason, it is not always necessary that every individual shake the hand of every other. Even when one or two people are introduced to a group, often a slight bow and a smiling hello will suffice.

Yes, this is ambiguous, and yes, there will always be that moment of plunging terror when you, as the one meeting the group, will be unsure as to whether to shake or not. Let them decide. If someone offers his hand, shake it. But once done, it should be repeated down the line, except for extreme cases, as when, e.g., someone is all the way at the other end of the conference table, deeply inaccessible in a restaurant banquette, etc. At such times, it's the thought that counts.

And don't forget: Whenever shaking hands, make eye contact. The worst handshaking no-no is to look over the shakee's shoulder (to see who just entered the room, for example) as you're shaking.

COMMON COURTESY BETWEEN THE SEXES

In General: Traditionally, some principles of etiquette have been quite useful, and others have been a pain in the neck. But when it came to interactions between men and women, back in the days when men were "men" and women were "women," a few could be pretty sexy. When, in *Now Voyager*, Paul Henreid placed two cigarettes in his mouth, lit them both, and then handed one to Bette Davis, everyone swooned. A man giving a woman a cigarette, and lighting it for her, had traditionally been a gesture rich in various kinds of symbolism: phallic and sexual (he's giving her a stick, then "setting her on fire" and making her "smoke"); mythic (he's presenting her the gifts of light and warmth); social (she's the passive recipient, he's the active performer); even economic (he's the producer, she's the consumer). When Henreid *put it in his mouth first*, he compounded and made doubly titillating the meaning and significance of an already highly charged act.

Today, of course (or "alas," to some), many women would find each of those symbolic meanings insulting and objectionable. Sexual liberation means no longer having to wait for a man to give you a cigarette (i.e., a "stick"); women are free to initiate their own social and sexual arrangements. Nor do they need a man to provide civilization's blessings, be they "the gifts of light and warmth" or anything else. Women are in all spheres of activity as active as men—particularly in the economic one. Like men, women are consumers; and, like men, they are producers, in every field.

Add to this another contemporary symbolic meaning, that a person offering you a cigarette is in effect inviting you to contract a fatal disease, and you end up with a once-dashing, courtly ritual of flirtation and politesse under indictment for extreme forms of social and medical rudeness. Is this progress?

It is not, if you lament the recent changes in women's social and economic roles, or if you think the Surgeon General more a party pooper than a guardian of the public health. On the other hand, it *is* for those at all sympathetic to "women's liberation" (even if they don't like to call it that), and those who believe that avoiding lung cancer by relinquishing cigarettes is a reasonable trade-off.

So now what? Are women still dainty, passive, and "pure," to be shielded from any physical action more arduous than batting eyelashes? Should men continue to be active, strong, and valorous enough to face the dangers of daily life, from a door which must be opened to a curb which must be patrolled?

"Neither," many would say, and go on to suggest that the whole two-part system be thrown out. Both sexes should be strong, active, and, like the redundantly described Wyatt Earp in the old television series, "brave, courageous, and bold." There should be no his-hers division of abilities or "essential qualities" for grown-ups.

Fine. The last thing *Mayflower Manners* wants to do is

COMMON COURTESY BETWEEN THE SEXES: A GUIDE FOR MEN

Old Way	New Business Way	New Social Way	Inherently Insulting?
Standing when woman enters room.	Nix, if she is inferior. Do it, if peer or superior.	Do it.	No.[1]
Standing when woman leaves room.	Only if she is superior.	Do it.	No.[2]
Lighting her cigarette.	Nix. Hints at flirtation.	Optional. Err on side of nix.	Inherently sexy, but w/ some BDO.[3]
Walking on curb side of pavement.	Optional if inferior, peer. If superior, err on side of yes.	Optional.	If raining, no. If not, a little.[4]

Holding coat as she puts it on.	Only for peer.	Optional. Err on side of yes.	Sort of.[5]
Opening, holding a door.	Optional.	Optional; err on side of yes.	No.[6]
Ordering at restaurant.	Nix.	Optional.	No, but—[7]
Giving her seat on bus, train.	Optional.	Optional, except in case of obvious need.	No.[8]
Carrying luggage in airport, hotel.	Nix, except for retrieving heavy bag from overhead.	Optional, but be sure to ask.	Maybe.[9]
Allowing her to go first into room, down corridor.	Nix for inferior; OK for others.	Do it.	No.[10]

to get into an argument over which qualities are inherent, or learned, by either sex. But even if you banish that old sex-based division of etiquette, you end up with a new two-part division—one of context rather than people, of setting instead of actors. Today, when men are men and women are women and both are consenting adults, politeness depends on where the interaction takes place: **Is it business, *or* is it social?**

Is *this* progress? *Mayflower Manners* prefers not to say one way or the other. It is content with the knowledge that it's just this sort of confusion that keeps etiquette writers in business.

COME ON, BABY, DON'T LIGHT MY FIRE

All **those old-time displays of courtesy**: Are they still necessary? Are they harmless, insulting, or especially pleasing? When a man holds a door open for a woman, should he get ignored, slapped, or extra credit?

Answers appear on the following chart. The traditional act of courtesy is followed by its new variation in business and its new form (if there is one) in social situations. Each entry includes a short comment about whether the act itself is inherently insulting to women, footnoted to a more lengthy discussion. Note that some answers are a disappointing, seemingly wishy-washy "Optional." Sorry. But we are dealing here with a highly complex sociological organism, not a flashlight that is either on or off.

Men tempted to memorize the chart completely are welcome to do so, but should also be advised that they may nonetheless still find themselves in awkward situations, i.e., dealing with a woman with her own sense of what and what not is to be done by you and by herself.

In the continually evolving dance of man-woman etiquette, it always takes two to tango. Therefore, when in doubt (even after consulting this chart), ask. If you want to open a door, but wish not to give offense, murmur "May I . . . ?" and permit her to answer either "Thank you" or "Oh, that's not necessary." If, after all that, she's still insulted, you've learned a valuable lesson about her.

NOTES

Inferior = someone at work whose position is inferior to your own

Peer = someone at work whose position, if not ability, is essentially equal to your own

Superior = someone at work whose position is above yours, however undeservedly

N.B.: "Optional" is not a fainthearted way of avoiding the issue. In all cases, the old rule was, Do It. The fact that some courtesies are now Optional affords men some leeway for the first time since the Middle Ages. It also, admittedly, affords them some new opportunities for anxiety and frantic self-examination. But isn't that what modern life is all about?

1. Note the two distinct motives and messages of traditional small courtesies: one implies the woman "can't" do something for herself, while the other simply shows deference and respect. This is an example of the latter. How, traditionally, have women shown "deference and respect" for men? By condescending to talk to them. No, it's not fair; hence these new rules.

2. See No. 1 above. Obviously, if you are enjoying a tête-à-tête in a living room, and she rises to answer the phone, you needn't stand. Use common sense.

3. BDO—"Big Daddy Overtones," or paternalistic im-

plications that the man is "taking care of" the woman. These are to be avoided.

4. Talk about old-fashioned! The original intent was to shield women from the garbage thrown out of upper-story windows overlooking the street. Today, of course, we have eliminated such distasteful practices, and instead strew the curb with garbage from street-level itself. Even so, things aren't as bad as they used to be. You might offer to guard the lady against being splashed after a heavy rain, but you might also think to guard yourself, and keep to the inner side of the sidewalk. If the curbs are dry, though, there is no reason to assume a woman cannot walk on the curb side. Is that what they mean by "a walk on the wild side"? It depends on the neighborhood, presumably.

5. Yes, it is inherently insulting—*to the man*, if he is holding the coat of his professional superior. But if he's holding it for a peer, or an inferior, then it's simple courtesy.

6. "Door," of course, means many things. Most women today appreciate a man's opening a car door when boarding a car or cab, but few still sit and wait for him to dash around and open it for getting out. They do it themselves. Doors to modern buildings, with their thick glass, pneumatic or other closing mechanisms, and panic-bar attachments, can be heavy objects, labor-intensive to open even for men. The cavalier who expects to sweep one open and hold it there with a single arm, as he gestures smoothly with the other, will find himself wrenching a shoulder. In the presence of such portals, suavity is beside the point: you push with both hands like a galley slave, walk the door into the open position, and hold it there as milady passes through. If you think that's humiliating, see "As the Door Turns," below.

7. This is tricky. One source, a woman, said that a gentleman born before 1945 living in urban areas will assume that he

should convey the lady's order to the waiter, and that she assumed it as well. Even when she needed to ask the waiter a question about a particular dish, she said, she would do so and then inform her companion what she wanted. He would then place the order.

Another source, a man born after 1945, assumed the opposite, viz., that women today would indeed find a man's ordering for them "inherently insulting," and would order their own meals. He noted, however, that this practice, like almost every other one on this chart, is in some sense arbitrary, that women offended by a man's ordering dinner for them might be delighted to have that man hold their coat, even if they are capable of putting it on unassisted.

There is a way out. Men: Look to the woman to signal you as to whether she expects you to do the ordering. Women: If your companion assumes he will do it, and you wish to order your own meal, you may, when he asks what you will have, express uncertainty. Wait until the waiter arrives, and then ask him some cursory question (to get his attention). Once the dialogue between you and him has been established, follow up briskly with your order. Your companion may be surprised, but it is doubtful he would be offended.

All this applies to social dining. The complexities of business dining, in which each party occupies a clearly defined position on a power gradient, make it inappropriate for a man to order for a woman.

8. "Obvious need" means, obviously, if the woman is elderly, pregnant, overburdened with packages and/or children, and so forth. Unfortunately, there will always be situations of uncertainty, when a fiftyish woman, hale and hearty and tough as a buzzard, will stand over you on a bus, sporadically glaring at you in an effort to bully or shame you into giving up your seat. A man can be forgiven at such times for thinking, "This

woman will outlive both her husband and me. They want free-dom and equality? They can stand for a few blocks." Such sentiments are understandable but, really, not very nice.

The law—i.e., *Mayflower Manners*— is sympathetic, however. Although in the end you should probably cave in, it offers you a way to at least neutralize her extortionate attitude. Smile at her, and ask to her face, "Pardon me, but would you like my seat?" If she says no, you're home free. If she says yes, at least you've made her acknowledge it. And who knows, maybe she'll say "please" and "thank you," which helps.

Ladies, this is a two-way street: If a man stands there with an armful of packages (or kids!), you should give him your seat. He'll feel thankful and you'll feel manly—which is to say, independent, strong, and able to stand on your own two feet.

9. This holds mainly for situations where bellboys, por-ters, or skycaps are unavailable. Offer assistance, and listen for its acceptance or refusal. Luggage is personal and besides, many women, especially those travelling on business, take it as a point of personal pride and professionalism to be able to carry, hoist, and retrieve their own.

10. Allowing a woman to precede you into a room, a res-taurant, etc., is a rather courtly gesture of deference, but don't worry—it's still okay. One key exception, though, is when she visits your office and is unfamiliar with the layout. You meet her at the reception area. You offer to "escort" her to your own office, or the conference room, or whatever. And you permit her to go first. She thereupon commences to blunder and hes-itate until you give her explicit directions where to turn, when to stop, etc.

This is nonsense. Etiquette, and even dignity itself, suffer when a lady is asked to go first down a hallway toward an utterly unknown destination. She becomes like a horse harnessed to a carriage, with you the driver murmuring instructions. Instead, think of these situations as a kind of office-dance. You lead.

AS THE DOOR TURNS

And then there are **revolving doors**. Who goes first and who does what? If the lady is permitted to go first, is she then expected to do all the pushing? Some of the pushing? And if she is not expected to push, yet still goes first, won't she be at the mercy of the strength and tempo of the push of the man behind her, thus subjecting her to being slammed in the back or the heels of her shoes by a door whose pace she cannot predict? But surely this cannot mean that she joins the man in untoward intimacy in a single chamber. Does, then, the man go first? But then, is not the woman required to time her entry into the door with split-second accuracy, as though leaping aboard a moving merry-go-round?

What fun—and all this to keep warm or air-conditioned air from escaping the lobby into the street. But there is an answer, and a very satisfying one at that. It embodies all the best points of contemporary social change and, by extension, of *Mayflower Manners*, i.e., courtesy, mutual respect, and cooperation. Men and women approaching the fearsome blades of a revolving door are advised to follow this simple three-step procedure:

1. The lady enters first, and starts pushing—slowly.
2. The man enters and also pushes.
3. Both push until the lady exits, and then the man.

All the above formula requires is that the lady and the man find a workable compromise between their two styles of pushing. If that isn't a metaphor for man-woman relationships in the nineties and beyond, nothing is.

𝒫UBLIC PLACES

In General: **T**here are two kinds of "public places": those we pay directly to enter, such as buses, planes, and theaters, and those we pay indirectly to maintain, such as parks, beaches, streets, and sidewalks. Either can be fraught with manners problems, since both are arenas in which personal imperatives must be reconciled with public policy (i.e., law), and with the general civic spirit of cooperation and respect we all must learn either to cultivate, or to fake. (In the end, there may be no difference between cultivating good manners and faking them.)

These days, in large urban areas, our experience of public places has been transformed from one of appreciating civilization's victories (architecture, commerce, engineering, cultural diversity, etc.) to confronting its failures. We speak, of course, of the homeless.

It is no trivial thing to suggest that before anything else, the problem of dealing with the homeless is an etiquette problem. How can it be otherwise, when in their presence all our most basic social precepts are thrown into question? If they are not always polite—well, we know otherwise normal people like that; it's a failing one can live with. But their transgressions are much more fundamental. They don't keep themselves clean—and we are repelled. They don't have a "job"—and we wonder why. They don't even have a "real" place to live. They don't "do" anything, and, worse, they don't seem to *try.*

Previously, when they were "bums" living on "their"

Skid Row, we could ignore them. But now they are everywhere—i.e., in *our* public places—which itself is anything from an inconvenience to an outrage to an actual physical danger. (Who can be sure which?) We have to interact with them. How? Politely? But they seem to defy our most basic rules for living. Why "should" we be polite to them, when they seem to refuse to uphold their half of every social bargain, to a degree that stops barely short of outright criminality? In fact, maybe that's what they are: not legal criminals, but etiquette criminals. Let the reader to whom that sounds insufficiently grave ponder his own sense of outrage and indignation —his sense of being *wronged*—when someone is rude to him.

Obviously, *Mayflower Manners* is not the place for a thorough discussion of this subject. Suffice to say that unless one is in actual physical danger, it behooves one to be courteous to the homeless. It's not as easy as it sounds: They often send confusing or unreadable signals, and refuse to read our own signals. Still, the pathetic truth is that not only is politeness toward the homeless "correct" as regards the rules of good manners, but many experts assert that a normal interaction with someone— a simple conversational exchange rather than being shunned, ignored, or rebuked—would do many of them a world of good.

Politeness is no more a cure for homelessness than comfortable pajamas are for an illness. Still, the very act of trying to do and say the right thing may be the first step toward mitigating the social problem. (It is not their homelessness that frightens us, after all, but the threatening attitude so many have lately seemed to display.)

Admittedly, that would be dealing with symptoms, not the disease. The disease can only be cured politically. Meanwhile, as anyone who has ever taken a cold pill knows, symptomatic relief can be just fine.

WORKERS OF THE WORLD: BE NICE

At first blush, it would seem that feminism has had no effect on the classic pas de deux between a **woman walking down the street and a construction worker calling out comments to her.** But look again: The man's comments may be as salacious and invasive as ever, but sometimes the woman's response consists of something unthinkable a generation ago (i.e., her raising her middle finger in the traditional, universally understood gesture). The lady's desire to "fight back" when verbally abused is commendable, but, sadly, both halves of this dialogue are rude and ill-mannered. The fact that "he started it" does not make acceptable a hand signal that no lady (or gentleman) should be caught dead conveying, at least in public.

However, some women, if pressed, will confess to being flattered if a scaffold's worth of men offer appreciative remarks about their appearance, provided such commentary is not obscene or insulting. Of course, it almost always is, and in fact is often accompanied by "kissy-sucky" noises of a most disgusting, objectionable nature.

There is nothing polite one can, or need, say to kissy-sucky noises. Such abusive displays of rudeness (not to mention obscenity) fall outside the purview of etiquette itself, and can only be responded to by stonily ignoring them. But while not all street banter between the sexes is so crude and abhorrent, it doesn't exactly qualify as delightful repartee. Men and women on the street—meaning men or women working at legitimate outdoor jobs, and passersby—ought to be able to exchange words of appreciation and gratitude without the dialogue degenerating into schoolyard noises and profane insults. Could there be a way to conduct curbside flirtations politely, decorously, and with due respect for the women's dignity and the men's right to freedom of expression?

Possibly. The chart below is directed toward construction workers, but is intended also for street maintenance workers, firemen, policemen, telephone linemen, utility workers, and anyone else whose labor takes them outdoors for long periods of time and brings them into juxtaposition with women walking down the street. Its first column offers a series of approximations of what such men say. (Verbatim reproduction of such comments would require language much too raw and graphic for *Mayflower Manners*.) The next column provides a corrective, noting what they should say to convey largely the same meaning. Following that is a listing of what a typical self-respecting woman will want to say in response to the original, unprintable comment. The chart concludes with a suggestion of what she should say instead.

No doubt many readers will wish to photocopy this chart and present it to the construction workers, etc. they know, as a public service. If by providing this information, *Mayflower Manners* contributes in some small way to the improvement of street life in our larger urban areas, then it will be content with that fact alone, and will require no further thanks other than a small, token Pulitzer Prize.

CURBSIDE COMMENTS

Suggested Good Manners for Construction Workers and Their Targets

What You Want to Say	What You Should Say Instead	What She Wants to Say	What She Should Say Instead
"Yo, lookin' good, momma."	"Excuse me, but you are quite attractive."	"Buzz off, jerk."	"Thank you."[1]
"Hey, sweet thing, nice legs!"	"Excuse me, but those stockings [sic][2] are extremely flattering."	"Eat your heart out, creep."	"Thank you."
"Bounce 'em, baby!"	"Excuse me, but you are most fetchingly endowed."	"My breasts are none of your damn business."	"Thank you."

"Oh man, what I could do to you . . ."	"Excuse me, but do you have the time?"[3]	"Don't even look at me, you pig."	"Good morning!"[4]
"Hey, honey, let's have oral sex!"	"Excuse me, but what do you think of the architecture of this building?"	"Drop dead, dirtbag."	"Good afternoon!"[5]
"You know you want me to perform sodomy with you, right?"	"Excuse me, but mind you don't walk into these potholes."	"Shut up or I'll call a cop, you piece of scum."	"Thank you!"[6]

NOTES

1. This and all similar thank-yous in this column do not connote real gratitude on the woman's part, nor are they necessarily preludes to further conversation. Rather, it is suggested that the woman offer a cursory—yet polite—thanks, and keep walking.

2. "Stockings," because most men probably assume that what they see are stockings. Even *Mayflower Manners* would not ask a construction worker to say "panty hose."

3. Note the dramatic contrast between what the man wants to say and what he should say. This entry marks the shift in the man's remarks, from general aesthetic appreciation of the woman in question to actual hints at and suggestions of erotic activity. As in the rest of polite society, encounters intended to culminate in sexual congress are initiated via scrupulously irrelevant conversation. Hence the bland, somewhat hackneyed query about the time. Subsequent entries in that column— about architecture and street hazards—serve a similar purpose.

4. Note the exclamation point. This indicates that the remark should be made in as overwhelmingly cheery and perky a tone as possible. The idea is to convey a benign but impenetrable obliviousness of the speaker, his comments, the nature of the morning, or even if it is morning at all. (The remark is all the more effective if delivered at six in the evening.) If, after being thus neutralized, the speaker presses his case and calls out another comment, you may feel free to ignore it and keep walking. Mannerswise, you've done your bit.

5. See number 4 above.

6. See number 4 above.

THE CLOTHES UNMAKE THE MAN
Some women know that it doesn't take much to encourage a man loitering against a building to say something intrusive. Other women, however, like the attention

they get when they wear certain kinds of **provocative clothing**. Or, at least, some kinds of attention. Must they accept whatever the male world dishes out when they dress to express? We know there is an etiquette as regards dressing up; what about dressing down?

Unfortunately, it is a principle of public places that you reap twice as much as you sow. A woman not comfortable exciting rude comments from men should downplay her wardrobe accordingly. It's not that it isn't "polite" to flaunt your assets—although taken to extremes, it isn't—but rather, it sends the wrong signals.

As for what constitutes "provocative," that is a relative term. Still, one rule of thumb concerning any given garment might be: If you think it goes too far, it probably does. When in doubt, toss it out.

$\mathscr{S}$PORTS

In General $\mathscr{A}$ll sports have their distinctive principles of etiquette, distinguished from technical rules and regulations by the term "sportsmanship." The latter make the game possible, but the former make it civilized. It is a touching thing to see when one professional bruiser on a football field helps another to his feet, or when a grimly determined city kid on a basketball court keeps an opponent from crashing into a fence. At such moments, when the players "break character" as opponents and reveal themselves as individuals, you remember that sports are not pitched battles for survival, but voluntary exercises people agree to create for fun and/or profit.

However, some people's idea of fun is to make each game a pitched battle. One can see this quite commonly in after-work leagues, where the gotta-be-a-winner ethic that has thrived over the past decade in business, law, finance, etc., is brought, along with the softball bats or basketballs, from the office to the diamond or court (A doctoral thesis in behavioral psychology is waiting to be written about the differing playing styles of, say, a basketball team of lawyers versus one of accountants, arbitrageurs, technical crews, writers and editors, and so forth.)

Ironically, though, the very business and professional influences that prompt men to display rudeness and (as they say in football) "unsportsmanlike conduct" also provide for sportsmanship's return via the presence of women—not women as spectators (as though such men would tone down their unmannerly behavior and clean up their act because women were watching; the opposite is more probably true), but women as players.

Does this mean, as some believe, that women are a "civilizing" influence on men? Not necessarily. The men have to be "civilized" to begin with, in order to display that quality once a lady joins the team. Besides, you could just as easily argue that men, through sport, have a barbarizing influence on women.

BOYS AND GIRLS TOGETHER

The central conundrum of **mixed teams**, of course, is, **How much should the men "try"?** Start with the assumption that on a softball field where each team consists of eight to ten players, most of the men will be significantly better than most of the women. (Readers not inclined to grant that assumption receive extra credit for feminist dedication. They may also skip this discussion. It will only upset them.) Any man who has spent his youth playing on boys-only teams in the neighborhood, at school, summer camp, etc., knows the downshifting in athletic zeal he experiences when women appear, not on his team, but on the opposite one. (If his team includes women, but his opponent's does not, what suffers is not his athletic zeal, but his expectation of winning. Women may call this sexist, but is there a man out there who would deny it?) In one-to-one confrontations with a female opponent, should he go all out, in order to win (on the assumption that his male opponents will do the same vis-à-vis his female teammates)? Or is that unsporting?

This problem pertains to games with larger teams—

LADIES FIRST

Allowances Men Should Make in Sports When Women Are on the Other Team

S = *Softball* **B** = *Basketball* **V** = *Volleyball* **F** = *Football (probably touch)*

Sport	Occasion	Don't . . .	Instead, Let Her	But You May . . .
S	she tags you out at second, third, or home	slide or bang into her	catch ball and try to tag you	wave hands, make silly noises
S	She's up, you pitch	burn 'em in	hit the ball	catch it if she does
B	she has the ball	steal it with a single swipe	dribble or shoot	block passes, wave hands
B	rebound	box her out forcefully	vie for ball	come down with it yourself
B	after basket	press if she brings it up	bring ball past mid-court	harass, force turnover

B	you drive to hoop	charge or leap through her	beat hasty retreat	continue drive
V	you spike at her position	smash it down with maximum force	live, by aiming away from her	then smash with maximum force
F	you block for runner	level her with a push	remain standing	fence her off from runner
F	she runs with ball	claw and punch at ball to strip it	keep it	touch or tackle her, as appropriate
F	she is QB	bang into her to jar ball loose	keep or pass ball	down her
F	you cover, she receives	hold her shirt, etc.	try to catch ball	intercept or bat ball away

softball, basketball, and volleyball, for example. Tennis, on the other hand, provides for exactly this circumstance; "mixed doubles" has its own rules and manners. But the problem only really becomes acute in the case of a one-on-one matchup—when, say, a man guards a woman dribbling a basketball, or finds himself heading for home from third and confronted by a lady catcher holding—if only for the moment—the ball. It is easy for an athletic man to steal a basketball from, or block the shot of, most women. It is easy (if not painless) for a man to barrel into a lady catcher and jar the ball loose. Winning requires that he do so. Should he?

This is a pure sportsmanship question, and the answer is no. Such coed sporting events are almost always for fun—as opposed to professional, for a living—and for that reason must be played in a way that accommodates all the participants. For that reason, a man should dampen his aggressiveness and play not an entirely passive game (which provides no fun for the lady, either), but in such a way that permits her to play her game. Note, however, that there are ample opportunities in such games where men may and do go head-to-head with each other, at which time they may (and do) play full-throttle.

The preceding chart illustrates the point. For several sports, certain common plays or situations are described, after which is listed what a man ought to forebear doing himself, followed by a suggestion of what he should per-mit his female opponent to do. Then, to his relief, appears a suggestion of what he may do to salvage his own athletic self-respect.

*W*HEN FRIENDS
(OR THEIR WORK)
ARE FEATURED IN MEDIA

In General: *D*on't laugh. Even if in the future everyone will *not* be famous for fifteen minutes, everyone will know someone who is. And that someone is sure to call all his friends, colleagues, and relatives, and manage to slip into the conversation, "Well, I didn't see the paper today. I had to show up at the studio at six-thirty in the morning . . ." (Pause for query: "Which studio?") "Oh, it's nothing—the studio where they do 'A.M. [Albuquerque/Columbus/other city].' They wanted me to talk about [hypnotism/city planning/other profession]."

The pervasive, almost *promiscuous*, way in which people in our society become famous has brought about a relatively new form of etiquette crisis. Two useful metaphors for discussing this are disease and gifts. Fame is a sort of antidisease, a general condition in which you go about your business while assuming (and hoping) that others will have a reaction. (With disease, the reaction is sympathy. With fame, it's admiration, congratulation, envy—all that.)

But when fame leads to publicity, and you appear in the newspaper, on television, or on radio, it's as though you're presenting a version of yourself to the public. You're giving the world a gift. Whether or not strangers pay attention is hardly important (unless you're especially insecure or megalomaniacal), but friends . . . won't they gladly accept this present you've offered? After all, it's . . . you!

SCREENING YOUR FRIENDS

What if **your friend is on TV?** He calls you days in advance, not to formally request that you watch, but hinting broadly that if you're any kind of a pal, you will. (Say the occasion is his being interviewed on a talk show about his profession—this, as opposed to a segment on the late local news featuring his arrest for drug smuggling.) Do you "have to" watch? What do you say when you skip it, and he asks what you thought? For that matter, what do you say if you do watch, you thought he spoke like an idiot or looked like a fool, and he asks you how he was?

If he asks it as a favor, treat it as a favor, and respond as you would to any other personal request. But if, either explicitly or implicitly, he leaves it up to you, you are not obliged to watch. It is something he does for his own purposes; he would surely do it even if you were in jail, dead, or on Mars. Only a clinically certified narcissist would expect others to feel the same excitement he does over an event that mainly affects him. Of course, your friend may *be* a clinically certified narcissist—in which case you've dealt with this sort of thing before, and know too well how weak a weapon etiquette is for coping with it.

The principle remains the same if **your friend's work is being broadcast.** If he is a writer, director, composer, or performer, his work's appearance on television may be a more frequent and more significant event than his simple occasional thirty-second comment on the news. (If it's his work's first appearance on TV, the occasion is very significant, at least to him.) But again, unless he expressly asks a favor, the principles of etiquette do not require that you watch. Note that the principles of *friendship* might require it—but that's a different story, and not relevant, thank God, to the present discussion.

BLACK AND WHITE AND UNREAD ALL OVER

Now consider writers. Not screenwriters or television writers but print writers, *writer*-writers, whose work, though far less glamorous than their movie or TV counterparts, is at least not remotely as lucrative. Your friend or acquaintance has **an article due to appear in a newspaper or magazine, or a book whose publication is imminent. "Must" you read it?**

Again, note that we distinguish between etiquette and what passes between friends. No sensible writer will expect, in the sense of requiring, that a casual acquaintance will read his work. Such an assumption would require the same sort of narcissistic personality alluded to above, in which case the writer would probably not be a writer at all, but an actor.

If you are a friend, the writer is justified in expecting you to read it only on a personal basis—if, that is, he knows that you know that the work is of extraordinary importance to him. And even then, his expectation should be mitigated by the accessibility of the work. An article in a newspaper becomes difficult to get a day or two after its appearance, a magazine piece threatens to disappear after a month (or a week), and so forth. If you failed to read the work, and encounter its author, a brief "I missed your piece. I'll try to hunt it down," will be sufficient. Everybody, including (especially) the author, fails to read things they feel they ought to. He will be poignantly grateful for your offer to seek it out, regardless of how cursory it sounds, and is. If he offers to send you a copy, you're stuck, but then the matter has escalated to a semi-formal request.

And, of course, if you are a fellow writer, you are both more likely to read it (out of professional interest) and less likely (out of professional boredom). You will be, respectively, thanked or forgiven, but almost never condemned, since the writer has probably been reading and/or neglecting your work for precisely the same reasons.

The only thing no one should ever say to a writer is a succinct "I read your [article/column/book]," with no elaboration. It sounds either coy (implying "and guess what my reaction was . . .") or, worse, as though you're expecting his gratitude and applause. (An even more objectional comment is "I saw your . . ." The writer will most likely take that at face value, and may even reply, with touching earnestness, "Great! Did you read it?")

Tell him you liked it, hated it, agreed, disagreed, whatever. Be aware that while the writer is sincerely curious as to your reaction, he does not want to have to coax it out of you by asking, "So? What did you think of it?" He's not *that* curious, and besides, he has his own, possibly tortured history with the piece in question. By the time it reaches print, it has gone through revisions, editorial comment, galleys, challenges, and discussions. The version you read may be a far cry from the one he originally intended. It may feature revisions with which he had nothing to do, to which he strongly objected, and so forth. To present yourself to him as another critic with an opinion, for which he must make a formal request, is the opposite of a kindness.

In return, you get the right to not read it if you don't want to.

$\mathcal{P}$ERFORMANCES

In General: $\mathcal{A}$ Night(mare) on the Town

Lance and Nancy are young, single, and in love. And they are on a date: Lance has managed to secure orchestra tickets (@ $50 each) to *Yes I Kan*, the lavish new Andrew Lloyd Webber musical "inspired" by the life of the German philosopher Immanuel Kant. Here is what transpires:

They arrive at promptly fifteen minutes after curtain time[1]—the overture has barely begun—and take their seats. Nancy's, it develops, is squarely behind a woman possessing a hairdo like an ayatollah's turban. Lance thoughtfully offers to trade seats with her, and she agrees. He will spend the entire evening shifting back and forth, trying to see around the woman's hair.[2]

Nancy settles into her now-unobstructed seat, and wonders: Is it the excitement of the moment that causes her to feel a sharp jolt at the base of her spine? No, it is the man behind her, attempting to shift to a comfortable position and banging his feet into the back of her seat. She turns in annoyance and snaps, "Do you *mind*?"[3] But the show is starting, and excitement fills the air. To her left, an elderly woman reads aloud from the playbill to her nodding companion, modulating her nasal drone in accordance with the volume of the orchestra. Nancy is thus able not to miss a single word of the credits of the show's assistant choreographer.[4]

The overture ends. The star, Len Cariou, strides out

to wild applause for his opening soliloquy. It is at that moment that the gentleman to Lance's right, regrettably mistaking the event for a motion picture, begins the elaborate unwrapping of a cellophane-covered box of chocolate-covered Brazil nuts. The incessant crinkling and crunching offers unwelcome competition to Cariou's thoughtful musings on the nature of human consciousness and the experience of love. Lance manages to hiss an emphatic "Will you SHUT! UP!"[5] when his attention is diverted by a woman two rows behind him, who yells, "Bravo!" as the star begins his song, "It's Categorically Imperative."[6]

The first act unfolds. There is comedy, romance, and drama, as Kant ponders the nature of ultimate reality. The companion to Nancy's elderly neighbor mutters, loudly, "I was in Königsberg in the war. It didn't look like that." Nancy rolls her eyes to heaven and issues a concise "Shh!"[7] A dramatic, full-scale production number brings the act to a close, after which there is widespread whistling and shouting.[8] The curtain comes down, the house lights come up. Intermission.

In the lobby, as Nancy repairs to the ladies' room, Lance stands in line for a bit of refreshment. Yet even the act of waiting proves to be stimulating, once a large, burly gentleman assumes a position in front of Lance, prompting him to tap the interloper smartly on the shoulder and say, "Hey. The end of the line is back *there*. Okay?"[9] The man leaves with a glare.

Nancy returns from the rest room with a crazy, inspired idea. They will find a pay phone, call a florist, and order a bouquet they will present to the costar of the show, Patti LuPone (Frau Kant). They do so, asking the delivery boy to meet them in the lobby just as the final number begins.

They are just able to reach their row as the lights dim for the second act. Asking those whose legs they must squeeze past to "watch it, please,"[10] they reach their seats as the curtain rises. Midway through the (somewhat more abstruse, theoretical) second act, both the elderly lady beside Nancy and her companion (her husband, presumably) fall asleep. Their percussive snoring provides an atmospheric counterpoint to the scenes depicting the hero's composition of his masterwork, *Critique of Pure Reason*. Nancy is careful to keep her eyes directed toward the stage as she jabs the snoozing lady with her left elbow and murmurs, "Come *on*. I can't *hear*."[11]

And then, alas, it is over. Kant's reputation is made, his influence on epistemology secure. As what is clearly the finale begins, Lance and Nancy leap up, gigglingly maul their way past those in their row not thoughtful enough to fold up their knees to their chests, and trot up the aisle.[12] In the lobby, a young man stands with a bouquet of roses. Lance takes it, tips him, and the pair wait in the rear of the auditorium until the curtain falls on the show and then rises again for the bows. The couple, scarcely able to contain their excitement, run at full tilt down the aisle, Lance's arms full of tissue-wrapped flowers, as Ms. LuPone takes her sweeping, triumphant curtain call.[13] (To do so, they must dodge and weave around those audience members opting to leave at that time.)[14]

They reach the lip of the stage. Lance holds out the flowers, obliging the startled Ms. LuPone to come forward and receive them as, in the audience, men and women yell, "Bravo!"[15] This she does, with gracious thanks. "Can we talk in your dressing room?"[16] Nancy asks— yells, actually—but the actress's attention has been diverted. No matter. When all is done, the pair wend their way backstage, tell the watchman, "We're friends of Patti's,"[17] and somehow gain access to the sanctum sanctorum. There, mingling among the thespians, friends, well-wishers, and others who actually have made the actress's acquaintance, they take in the atmosphere and praise the performance, in other productions on television and in movies, of everyone whom they recognize who may have been in that evening's show.[18]

Finally, they reluctantly allow themselves to be asked to leave by none other than Ms. LuPone herself.[19] They exit the theater via the stage entrance in a haze of wonder and satisfaction, agreeing that it has been a more or less perfect evening and asking the watchman to call them a cab.[20]

NOTES

1. Arriving fifteen minutes after curtain is dreadful. At many performances, such late arrivers would not be admitted until "a suitable break in the performance." Ticketholders should take literally the time noted on their tickets, and not consider it merely a helpful hint.

2. Even Lance knows that he could not very well ask the woman, "Madame, would you kindly remove your hair?" The next time he finds himself behind her, however, he could try dropping a polite hint: "Excuse me," he might say. "But I apologize if you hear me moving around a lot. It's just that I'm having a hard time seeing over your hair." Might this shame the lady into sitting further down in her seat? Probably not.

3. Nancy's exasperation is understandable, but hissing

rhetorical questions about minding is, at least technically, rude. She ought to have simply turned and looked at the man with an expectant expression, perhaps whispering an attentive "Yes?" With luck, this sudden (polite) confrontation would have alerted him to the problem.

4. All conversation should cease once the music or drama begins. Nancy might have reminded her neighbor of this obliquely, with something like "Excuse me, but I think the music is starting." This remark is all the more pointed if it is plain that the music has started ten minutes ago.

5. It is impossible to use the term "shut up" in any polite context. Fortunately, the wrapper-rattler is immediately adjacent to Lance, who is therefore able to respond with an icily insincere but outwardly impeccable "Excuse me. But do you need help with that?" Had the offender been farther away, Lance would have had to content himself with a withering stare, and the hope that the fellow's closer neighbors would offer their assistance.

6. Theatrical performances are not gospel services, in which the faithful may shout whatever they want whenever the spirit moves them. Bravos are best saved until after musical numbers, or at the end of acts.

7. Occasional remarks to one's partner are admissible, but only if they are discreetly whispered, kept brief, and do not result in a prolonged exchange. In reacting to the annoying conversation of others, a sharp shush is the easiest, but is, it must be said, impolite. Technically, Nancy should have whispered a formal request for the gentleman to please be quiet.

8. There is nothing wrong with whistling and shouting at the close of acts, providing the shouting is in the form either of preverbal gibberish ("WHOAAAAA!") or a Romance language ("Encore!" "Bravo!" etc.). This rule is waived at rock concerts, at which almost anything can be shouted at almost any time, in any language, except for those poignant moments when a lone performer sings to an acoustic guitar. And even

then. Note, however, that while at a rock concert it is appropriate to cry "Rock and roll!" at will, it is not appropriate at a musical comedy to shout "Musical comedy!" to bellow "Opera!" at an opera, etc.

9. Lance's exasperation is understandable, but he has forgotten the Primary Loophole of etiquette: You may say what you mean, if you do it deferentially. Thus, a preferable response might have been "Excuse me, but you may not be aware—the end of the line is back there." (N.B.: *Mayflower Manners* admits that such a comment offers a perfect setup for a rejoinder along the lines of "Yeah? Well, excuse me, but you may not be aware that you can kiss my—." Such a remark is rude.)

10. "Watch it, please" is impolite, as is returning to one's seat after Act II commences. Promptness, and a series of discreet excuse-mes, are preferable.

11. Nancy is better advised to wake the noisy sleeper with a shake of his or her arm and a concerned-sounding "Excuse me, but are you all right?"

12. Having to leave while a performance is in progress sometimes cannot be helped. Such exits are best done as rapidly and quietly as possible. Giggling as you stumble your way down the row is a bad way to do it.

13. To present a performer with flowers, do not hand them over yourself. Instead, call the theater before the performance, and get the address of the stage door entrance. The theater itself may be able to advise you on which florists it usually deals with. Have the arrangement sent to that door by the time you wish. Be sure it comes in a vase: The gift of flowers, normally so delightful, becomes an aggravating burden when an armful of (wet) plants is thrust upon you. Be sure to include a card, too.

14. As to leaving during the curtain call: Some condone it. *Mayflower Manners* thinks it's rude—to the audience members who want to applaud the actors as they take their bows, and

to the actors themselves. There are two basic reasons for walking out during the applause: for personal convenience, or out of dislike for the production. The first is irrelevant where manners are concerned—patrons encouraged to leave theaters early in order to catch trains or dismiss babysitters will next expect to be allowed to arrive late, due to tardy babysitters or inconvenient train schedules.

As for those disliking the production, patrons so disposed are advised to refrain from applauding. They may even yell "Boo" if so moved; it is a practice sanctified by theatrical tradition. But so is the curtain call. The play (or musical, opera, etc.) may be over when the curtain comes down, but the event is not. The house lights have not yet come up, and the performers are still on the stage. Indeed, to applaud a good production along with others is itself a public pleasure, and as such helps make going to the theater a different experience from watching something at home on television. Patrons leaving during the curtain call disrupt that experience.

Even the audience member who leaves at that time because she has a rendezvous with the tenor may take her time. The tenor is onstage, bowing.

15. One does not yell "Bravo" at or for Patti LuPone or any female performer. One yells "Brava." For a group of performers, one yells—if one dares—"Bravi."

16. An actress's public obligations are fulfilled once her role is played. She is not obliged to receive strangers for postmortem sessions in her dressing room. Once the curtain calls are over, she is a private person, at least nominally.

17. This is a lie, and could conceivably cause the watchman to get into trouble. See number 16 above. Also, it should not be assumed that any performer is free to receive guests after a show. They may, among other things, have to receive notes from the director. And as for visiting during intermission,

by all means check with the actor beforehand. Some enjoy it, and some find it deeply distracting.

18. Actors, like everyone else, love praise. They may even love it a little more than everyone else—indeed, more than everyone else put together. Still, the handsome thing to do when praising an actor after a play is to do so with reference to the role just performed. If, after that, you wish to discuss their other work, be their guest.

19. Lance and Nancy have fallen victim to the Touristic Fallacy, so named and explained specifically by *Mayflower Manners* here for the first time, exclusively for the purposes of its publication. It consists in assuming that since this is your first day in Rome, then it must be the first day too for all the Romans you meet. Mutatis mutandis, since this is Lance and Nancy's first time for seeing *Yes I Kan*, it must be Patti LuPone's first performance of it also. It isn't. What is a gala and festive event for the audience is usually just another night's work for the actors, with the exception of landmark performances such as openings, closings, etc. Therefore the couple should have kept their (unauthorized, uninvited) visit to a minimum, and not waited to be the last ones to leave save the "hostess."

20. The watchman at a stage door is not a doorman lacking a spiffy overcoat. Call your own cab.

IN
PRIVATE

THE
BACHELOR DWELLING

In General: You would think that in these days of post-feminist enlightenment, when men are "allowed" to pay attention to such things as decor, cooking, and sprucing up their wardrobes, that the old-time, all-thumbs, domestically inept bachelor would be a creature of the past. You would think such a fellow had his heyday thirty years ago, when men were men and women were "girls," and furnishing an apartment, broiling a lamb chop, or selecting a tie were just too sissified for words—or, were skills to be learned from magazines like *Playboy* and *Esquire*, solely for the (redeeming) purpose of seduction.

You would think that, and you would be wrong. That kind of man is still with us, still secretly (or openly) believing that his inability to bake a chicken without burning down his high rise proves something admirable about his masculinity. (Sooner or later he will marry a "girl" whose inability to bake a chicken without burning down their high rise will inspire him to make jokes about her incompetence and stupidity.) His apartment is a place of paradox: The kitchen, which he hardly ever uses, is nonetheless a shambles, and can qualify for EPA Superfund disbursements. The bedroom, avowedly a site of maximum comfort and luxurious indulgence, can resemble a student's dorm during Finals week. And often what is not there is as upsetting as what is—the ratio of bottles of imported beer in the fridge to clean drinking glasses in the cupboard can be a dismaying six to zero.

It's not for *Mayflower Manners* to explain how to keep an apartment or townhouse well stocked and tidy. (Magazines like *Playboy* and *Esquire*, or one's mother, do that rather well.) However, the following can provide a sense of what essential items the above-described bachelor should make available to his (various categories of) guests. And let there be no fretting or second-guessing about the validity of the information—it has been gleaned from discussions with actual men and women.

Does all this really qualify as "etiquette"? Let's say yes. Let's say that the underlying principle is that ancient manners-axiom, as old as civilization itself, which holds that a host is responsible for the comfort and safety of his guests. After that, the rest is detail.

A BACHELOR'S DEGREE IN HOME EC

To begin at the beginning: What **basic amenities and creature comforts** should the self- and guest-respecting bachelor provide? Well, surely it's not necessary to state that the entire place should be reasonably clean and tidy, is it? Oh dear. All right: The entire place should be reasonably clean and tidy. In fact, female sources cited this as the most significant hazard encountered in visiting a bachelor's home. (Lucky them; all male-female problems should be so easily solved.) Male sources, on the other hand, thought that a good stereo and cable TV (duly equipped to receive the major sports channels) were the highest priority.

Note here that both male and female sources were asked questions pertaining to the same thing, i.e., an unmarried man's home. Thus, when women responded, it was in terms of what they hoped they'd find when visiting a man's place. Men, on the other hand, discussed what *they themselves* deemed essential for their own dwellings. Not surprisingly, requirements varied according to sex. Women were insistent that toilet paper is no substitute for Kleenex (although both are necessary), while men demanded beer in bottles, not cans, and snacks. Women liked diet soda; men insisted on a comfortable place to sit while watching TV. Women wanted clean hand towels. Some men expressed a desire for particular brands of liquor.

Get the picture? What's essential to the host is deemed irrelevant by the guest—a surefire recipe for those nagging, superficial-but-nonetheless irritating feelings of grievance that arise when an etiquette misdemeanor has been committed. Therefore, male readers, take note of this and what follows: Your visitors are seldom content simply to make do with whatever meager domestic provisions you, in your manly obliviousness, have provided. "But," someone will protest, "I thought **a man's home is his castle**. Isn't my apartment **the one place I can keep as I see fit**? Isn't it just too bad if lady visitors don't like it? Isn't a person's home an expression of himself, of his personality?"

In a word, no. It's not that simple. Each of us has, in general terms, two personalities, or two aspects to a single complex personality. One is personal, the other social. True, hermits living by themselves in conditions of unremitting squalor do "express" the personal aspects of themselves while explicitly ignoring the social. But then, they're hermits; that's their job. You, presumably, are different. If you invite anyone at all to your home, that invitation constitutes a social act. In issuing it you volunteer, willingly, for the role of host, and assume all the obligations that go with it, as set forth in the rules of socializing (i.e., etiquette). In exchange for obeying them, you get the pleasures of polite, nonhermitlike human society.

"But **sometimes my visitors aren't really there to be 'guesty' kinds of guests**," this same someone will doggedly reply. "So why do I have to be a 'hosty' kind of host?" You don't, if by that you mean a formal entertainer and preparer of refreshments (i.e., a cook). Even if the reasons for the visitor's presence in your apartment are primarily sexual (i.e., not for socializing or romance), the point is that she is in *your* apartment, not her own. You may not have to cook for her, but you do owe her some basic amenities, beginning with cleanliness. (If you play your cards right, she may want to cook, taking pity either on you, for being unable to make a decent meal, or herself, for being unable to score one at your place. In either case, thank her, and pick up the tab. You're getting off easy.)

By the way, **if you do cook, does she have to do the dishes?** No, but she should offer. Just as you should, but probably don't, when she cooks for you at her place.

"You mean I have to do the dishes, too? But—"

No buts. Let's leave it with this: If you want to live like a disgusting slob, that's your right. But if you want someone else to come over, you have to (literally) clean up your act.

"Okay, okay. But when she comes to my place, and

has to be **buzzed in, do I have to go all the way down and meet her at the door?"**

Only if the buzzer doesn't work.

CHANGE THE SHEETS? BUT I JUST DID TWO WEEKS AGO . . .

Having provided the basics addressed above, you sit back, content that you've done your duty. You've bought a box of Kleenex and, sport that you are, you've even hung up a couple of small towels. The pressure's off. You're ready to buzz her in.

Not so fast. Woman does not live by Kleenex alone. The idea is to provide comfort, not just escape indictment by the Manners Police. Still, how far should you go? You and your companion could be anything from total strangers to lifelong soulmates. How to know who is entitled to what sort of **extra amenities**?

In considering this question, let there be two basic categories:

A BEDMATE will be defined as an occasional sexual partner with whom one is not having a "relationship." Yes, it *is* vague. But you know who you, and they, are. If you don't, perhaps it makes more sense when contrasted with—

A GIRLFRIEND, with whom one is having a relationship, even if not an exclusive one. (Again: all this is directed toward men, so there is no corresponding Boyfriend category. *Straight* men.)

Note that with this section we have moved from the living room, with its sports channel and diet soda, to the bedroom, with—well, with its sports channel, and diet

BEDMATES VS. GIRLFRIENDS: WHAT THEY EXPECT, WHAT THEY GET AT A BACHELOR'S HOME		
	What Women Say They Want	**What Men Assume They Must Provide**
Bedmates	Clean sheets Clean bathroom and fresh towels Shower cap Condoms	Relatively clean sheets[1] Towels[2] Condoms
Girlfriends	Clean sheets[3] Comfortable pillows[4] Fresh towels Shower cap Bathrobe Facial soap[5] "Decent" shampoo and conditioner Toothbrush Hair dryer Preferred beverage Coffee/tea for A.M.[6] Big T-shirt to sleep in Specific place to store gear Small amount of closet space, hangers Decent reading light in bed Selected reading matter[7]	Clean sheets[8] Fresh towels Some of her favorite foods

soda, but with much else besides. To explain what category of liaison is entitled to *tutti*, or less than *tutti*, *conforti*, the chart on the facing page.

NOTES

1. Footnotes already? Alas, yes. "Relatively" is here used loosely—very loosely. When applied to sheets, it means "clean enough that previous liaisons aren't obvious to the casual observer." What is a "casual observer" doing in the bedroom with the two of you? Good question.

2. Pretty depressing, isn't it? "Towels." Sources seemed to mean by this, "towels which have been used less than a week and have not just been picked up off the floor."

3. I.e., "which have not been slept in by another woman since they were last put on the bed."

4. In "sufficient number."

5. I.e., not a harsh deodorant soap.

6. Includes milk, sugar, Sweet 'N Low, and possibly even something to nibble on, e.g., English muffin, toast, etc.

7. Most sources admitted to leafing through a *Playboy* or *Penthouse* and enjoying it, but were put off by anything more . . . extreme. Articles often pave the way for discussing certain topics that may be difficult to bring up otherwise, e.g., Who's the best player in the NBA: Michael Jordan, or Magic Johnson?

8. Some men declared themselves scrupulously "considerate" about providing clean sheets. There are at least two possible explanations for this. One is that they are scrupulously considerate men. The other is that they are scrupulously careful about preventing a girlfriend from finding evidence of extracurricular activity.

The lessons to be learned from the preceding chart are profound. When thinking of themselves in the role of bedmate, women display an asceticism worthy of a

Zen monk. Linen, a clean bathroom, and various plastic/ rubberized forms of protection—prisoners on Death Row probably get more. (The only occasion when a bedmate expects **clean linen** is when the relationship has been long-standing, even if casual.)

And men are correspondingly willing to provide these things unasked—all except the shower cap, an understandable omission, since most men don't use one themselves. Consensus about clean linen varies among men, though. Younger men seem to adopt an attitude of "What you can't really see probably isn't really there." (Most of such sources do their own laundry, a reason for wanting to keep sheet washing to a minimum). While older men (over thirty) concede that they, too, probably wouldn't change sheets between bedmates unless "it was obvious," they rarely have multiple bedmates in a one-to-two-week period to begin with. All agreed that girlfriends merit clean linen.

As for those girlfriends: Once a woman attains that status, she requires things you'd be hard-pressed to find in a luxury hotel. ("Big T-shirt to sleep in"?) Men, though, hang tough. They omit the condoms (probably because once she's his "girlfriend," that matter has long been resolved), and substitute food. A lady pondering the ridiculous disproportion between the two lists (sixteen to three) might be excused for wondering if men can be bothered to make their girlfriends feel at home at all.

In fact, they can. All male sources said they'd willingly supply their girlfriends with whatever they wished, if they only knew. And, as we've seen in the first section above, men ask for their own homes only a sports channel, a couch, and some bottled beer. So women, rather than despairing (and feeling secretly superior) because their male hosts promote such bad housekeeping, should simply speak up.

Of course, all the above represents a gathering of opinions from the field. What does *Mayflower Manners* think? Can a man's home be a pigsty as long as he keeps in his refrigerator a can of Diet Pepsi and a shower cap? Or does he "have to" run out and buy all the things on a list handed triumphantly to him by his girlfriend?

Neither. **Basic bachelor dwelling etiquette** is simple and reasonable. Not negotiable is cleanliness, in every room and particularly bedroom and bathroom. Provide every new visitor with clean linen, and don't pretend you don't know that "linen" refers to sheets and towels even if they're cotton, flannel, silk, or cotton-poly blend, and aren't literally made of "linen." If you know beforehand that you will definitely, probably, or even possibly end up back at your place, change the sheets. (If you had no idea, and are caught with less than pristine linen, don't worry. The surprise and excitement of the moment will carry both of you through. The first time, anyway.)

Condoms, of course, are essential for any sexual relationship not monogamous over the last ten years. (See section on "Sex," below.) Pillows obviously. A man knowing that at some time or another in his life he will be entertaining women should keep a shower cap handy. As for all that other stuff, from the big T-shirt to the reading light, it doesn't seem all that unreasonable. She ought not to be offended if it isn't there; but he ought not to be miffed if she asks for it. If she's been visiting four or five times a month or more, she may **request** that he stock her favorite soda, snacks, contact lens solution, etc. Dare she? Yes, provided she does not simply expect him to without her asking. Love is one thing; being able to read someone's mind is another. If he fails to pick up subtle little hints, she should go with him to the store, drop the stuff she wants in the basket, and offer to split the cost.

ALONE AT LAST

With the developing relationship comes trust; soon you are comfortable leaving her alone in your formerly sacrosanct dwelling as you depart early for work or return late from the health club. She has a key. She's all by herself in your home.

And the phone rings. **Should she answer?**

Most male sources said no, and indeed, it seems a presumption for a woman to answer a man's phone in his absence (and vice versa) unless the relationship has attained a mutually acknowledged level of seriousness. Besides, by now most people will have a phone machine, rendering the question moot. But if you do answer, and hear the voice of a woman whom you take to be (an unknown, unauthorized) rival, think twice before **confronting your lover** with a question. You are entitled to know about only those parts of his life about which he chooses to tell you. (And, again, vice versa.) Unless he has asked you to answer the phone, you are harboring illegally obtained "evidence" that might not, in fact, be proof of any "crime" whatsoever.

Your revelation of it, though, will be seen for the breach of trust that it is. If he is indeed guilty of violating the terms of your relationship, your having caught him via

snooping will only make matters worse. True, by that
point, you may not care. But if he is not guilty, your
having pried will become the crime of the moment, and
he will have cause to accuse and condemn you. It's bad
manners to snoop, in someone's mail, on someone's phone,
or in any other way. And even if you believe that what's
at stake is more important than "manners," bear in mind
that your spying, once revealed, could do more harm to
the relationship than anything it might uncover.

Of course, it's easy to let ringing phones lie, since they
always include a third party able to bear witness to your
snooping. **Going through someone else's drawers and
other private effects** is another matter. How do you, as
the absent, snooped-on male, handle it if you believe
you will be, or have been, investigated without your
consent?

This too is a delicate matter, since one doesn't want
to accuse another of a crime of which she may not be
guilty. One solution is to accuse or warn in a general,
pro forma way, which you can disavow if it is brought to
your attention. We speak here of the ever-useful General
Warning. You might leave, in sensitive strongboxes or
drawers containing classified documents, a note (preferably written on old-looking paper, so as not to seem
done yesterday), with the warning TO WHOM IT MAY
CONCERN: SNOOPING IN THIS AREA STRICTLY
PROHIBITED, or something to that effect. You thus
make the point while retaining absolute deniability:

"I found this note while looking for a [harmless ob-
ject]," she says to you that evening. "What's the matter?
Don't you trust me?"

"Oh, that . . ." you smile with slight amusement. "I

put that there last year, when I was involved with [remote person or made-up name]. That's not meant for *you*."

Note that you are able to discover that she has snooped while ostensibly complimenting her trustworthiness. Whether you believe that she indeed was only looking for [harmless object], or not, is your next problem.

Of course, all problems can be avoided by keeping sensitive documents, photographs, garter belts, etc. in a secure form of storage—a locked box, a safe-deposit, etc.

One final comment: As mentioned above, it is always risky to reveal knowledge you are not "supposed" to have. The very fact of your having it announces both mistrust on your part and a willingness to invade the other's privacy. If you do snoop, and **you do discover classified information**, it is absolutely inadmissible to use such information in quarrels—not only because "it's bad manners," but because it can be lethally self-defeating. It leads to accusations, not about specific issues, but about general character, and can quickly escalate into the interpersonal equivalent of nuclear war: the use of all-or-nothing weapons, not to defeat the "enemy," but to destroy him altogether. No relationship can survive such an exchange.

THE MESSAGE IS THE MEDIUM

As mentioned above, phone machines often eliminate the temptation to answer an absent partner's phone—although they replace it with the temptation to listen in on the monitor to hear who's calling and what they say. (This, too, is snooping, and subject to the above restrictions.) But now say the two of you arrive at your apartment after a day or night out, and discover several messages have been left on the machine. **Is it rude of you to play them back in her presence?**

Yes, if you have reason to suspect that any of the messages would be embarrassing (or worse) for her to hear. If you're sure you have "nothing to hide," go ahead. But if you think (or hope) that there might be something best addressed to your ears only, wait until she leaves the room.

HIDE IN PLAIN SIGHT

And then there are **condoms**. Or, if there aren't, there should be, for reasons to be discussed later. What arises now is the homemaking aspect of using them, i.e., **Is it rude, pushy, or otherwise objectionable to leave them in view in the bedroom?**

You can see why it might be. Condoms left out brazenly in the open might signal any one of several impolite—not to say ludicrously macho—attitudes:

CONDOMS ON DISPLAY: WHAT IT IMPLIES

1. I use these things so damn much I keep 'em handy all the time. That's how popular I am.

2. I just used these things recently (i.e., with someone else), and forgot to put 'em away. That's how popular I am.

3. I have these things because I'm a sexual kinda guy, so hey—wanna use one?

4. I make use of these items because I am, let me assure you, extremely sensitive to the possible dangers (to *either* partner) of unprotected intercourse in today's

tragically disease-haunted society, so hey—wanna use one?

Naturally, female readers of *Mayflower Manners* would never be so wanting in taste (or desperate) to wind up in the bedroom of a man capable of the above sentiments . . . but still. Is it okay to leave them out?

Sources in the field had contrasting reactions. Some women did indeed find it distasteful to see them out in the open. But others found it a relief to know—without having to resort to discussion—that the man had them and, presumably, would be using them. Very few men actually did leave them out, and said they did so for exactly that reason.

Those men who kept them concealed did so for two sharply divergent motives. One was the (praiseworthy) feeling that displaying them was distasteful. The other was the (less praiseworthy) hope that hiding them would lessen the possibility that they would be asked to use them.

This latter is a case of a good act for a bad reason. Condoms are best kept in a convenient drawer or box— convenient, that is, to wherever you might have sex. The uncertainty a woman might feel in not seeing them right away is compensated for by the absence of pressure she might feel were they staring her in the face. Besides, her worry can be alleviated by the good manners of her companion, who will acknowledge their necessity when, or rather, just before, the time comes.

BATHROOM

In General: With the possible exception of prison, the bathroom is the last place one wants to have to worry about the do's and don'ts (or, rather, the please-do's and kindly-don'ts) of etiquette. After all, one way to look at etiquette itself is as a system of rules and guidelines for conduct between strangers. Good manners is how strangers demonstrate, or approximate, or at least temporarily fake, respect for one another.

Yet the bathroom, at least in the home, is usually devoid of strangers. (An exception might be when you host a large party. Then guests you have invited often arrive accompanied by a delightful variety of friends, visitors from out of town, guys and/or gals from the office, and simpatico acquaintances, met not three minutes before in the elevator, whom you have not laid eyes on before, let alone invited. But even then, such groups tend not to congregate in the bathroom.)

However, there comes a time in a relationship between a man and a woman when one finds himself or herself in . . . how to put it? . . . the other's bathroom. And certain ambiguities inevitably arise, based on the question of whether the room is essentially public or private. Assuming that one's home is, of course, ultimately and absolutely private, the distinction still has meaning. The living room, for example, is a public space, while the bedroom is private. However, few hosts are lucky enough to be able to offer their guests the use of a "powder room," i.e., a bathroom designated for use by the public (for a now-obsolete 1970s connotation, see "A Toot and a Whistle," below). And of those powder rooms that are available, few are equipped with a shower. Sooner or later, therefore, everyone finds themselves alone in another person's most personal, intimate chamber.

One looks around and wonders, What are the rules? If this zone is so private, a man thinks, what are all her intimate, fascinating, frightening unguents and potions doing in plain view behind this easily-opened medicine cabinet door? If this room is indeed public, a lady muses, why does he bother to conceal his personal salves and prescriptions behind this noisy, squeaking medicine cabinet door?

A discussion of bathrooms, then, is not only in order, but essential. If *Mayflower Manners* promises it won't be salacious or embarrassing, will you read it anyway?

To start, the inevitable . . .

SECRETS OF THE MEDICINE CABINET

Let's not be disingenuous, or at least not until we're caught red-handed. The **medicine cabinet** is a private cache. This fact is signalled, as it is in other areas of the home, by a device known as a "door." Just as you would never dream of entering, without receiving permission, a room in another's home to which the door was shut, so should you never dream of peeking behind that mirrored portal. Oh, all right, go ahead and dream about it. But if you actually do it, and are found out, you should be prepared to justify the intrusion. Memorize the tables below. The first provides you with a series of excuses, some more plausible than others. The second equips you to anticipate a sensible person's objections to the lame excuses you picked up from the first table.

So much for the more common excuses for prying into a host's medicine chest. Note that they're all "practical," as are their refutations. But if you still need reasons why you shouldn't be peeking behind the mirrored door, here are two ruthlessly impractical but utterly central ones.

The first: It's not polite.

The other is, you might discover minor but off-putting things you'll wish you hadn't: unappetizing allergies, disillusioning hair dyes, ominous chronic diseases, etc. These are intensely personal items, ones which your host will reveal to you when and if he/she sees fit.

And if you discovered a prescription drug made out to an unknown person of the opposite sex, what then? Never quite certain who the person is (a lover? a friend? a relative?), you'd probably be both glad you found out and wishing you hadn't. You certainly couldn't work a question about the bottle's owner into the conversation without seeming at best a snoop, at worst an invader of privacy. (The difference: A snoop pries into things that he or she will probably find out in time, legitimately. An invader of privacy trespasses where he or she would probably never be invited.)

Still tempted? Oh dear. In that case, staring at that image in the mirror, which is of yourself contemplating betraying a minor but real trust, remember this: If you are in that person's home in search of romance, you won't find it in the medicine cabinet. Instead, if you peek, you'll find its opposite, which is knowledge. Now, knowledge is all well and good, of course—but don't you get enough of it from the rest of the world?

LOOKING IN OTHER PEOPLE'S MEDICINE CABINETS:

Table I: Blameless Justifications

1. I was looking for something.
2. I want to make sure I'm not getting involved with someone suffering from chronic headaches or upset stomachs.
3. I want to see what kind of birth control she uses, so we don't actually have to discuss it.
4. I'm in advertising/marketing/product development/etc., and like to see what brands my host/hostess buys.
5. I like to check out products I've never used before.
6. I want to make sure I'm not getting involved with someone addicted to prescription drugs.
7. I want to see if another woman/man is keeping her/his personal effects here.

Table II: Decisive Objections to Blameless Justifications (numbers correspond to entries in Table I)

1. What sort of "something"? Everything you legitimately need is out on the sink.
2. How could you tell? By the presence of aspirin or Tums? Please.
3. There are other ways of finding out, and what's wrong with discussing it? Besides, its presence in the cabinet is no guarantee that she'll actually use it, so you'd be forced to ask anyway.
4. A likely story. Either ask, or confine such clandestine field research to the kitchen.
5. What a good idea. Why not slip out and borrow your host's car, too, while you're at it?

6. If they're prescription, they could have a legitimate use. How could you detect addiction? "I couldn't help but notice Percodan in your medicine cabinet. If you don't mind my asking . . . are you addicted?" Try that, and note how pleased your host will be that you asked.
7. If your relationship permits you to ask instead of snoop, why bother snooping? And if it doesn't, then the whole thing is none of your business.

INTRODUCTION TO BASIC

Having assured, with the above argument, that visitors will not violate the sanctity of the medicine cabinet, or will not tell us if they do, we are ready to attend to their needs. **What basic equipment** should a host provide for "the public" in his or her bathroom? The answer sounds like a personal hygiene kit distributed to refugees in a war zone, but then, human needs are basic the world over: soap, a towel, a box of tissues, and toilet paper. Add, for extra credit, the relative luxuries of hand cream, mouthwash, and good lighting.

Accessories aside, it is your **duty as host** to assure that the bathroom be as clean as possible before a guest arrives. Unfortunately, "clean" proves to be a highly subjective term. Most sources, however, agreed that the list of items it is essential to keep tidy include the sink, the toilet, and the mirror. A clean tub, for men, seemed more a theoretical ideal to which one might aspire, while to women it was a necessity: Of those sources consulted, nearly all the women, but none of the men, admitted to peeking behind the shower curtain and/or taking notice of the bathroom's floors and corners.

Note, too, that tissue is more important to women than to men; bachelors therefore should remember that toilet paper is not an acceptable substitute. And most sources disapprove of blue or green water in what television commercials call "the bathroom bowl." Many consider it thoughtful to provide current or unusual reading material, which emphatically does not include books of "jokes" specifically created for that purpose. Another thoughtful/ shrewd inclusion is a book of matches to help clear the air. It provides a cheap and effective alternative to leaving the door closed, which does nothing at all except prepare a knockout blow to fell the next person who walks in.

WRINGING YOUR HANDS OVER THE SOAPS
They're lovely, those **guest soaps** like sculptures of marzipan, those **guest towels** that seem like . . . well, towels, but not of the sort one can actually use for *drying* anything. Or can one?

Absolutely. Indeed, an example of the confusion over bathroom etiquette can be seen in the hesitancy and intimidation one feels in the presence of these silly little things. They seem too delicate and formal and *nice* for the relatively crude, banal activity of drying the hands. (Interestingly, this sort of conflict never arises over, say, sterling silver dinnerware, which looks more imposing and pristine, costs much more, and is put to a far more intimate use.) Not everything connected with etiquette is intuitively sensible, but here is one principle that is: Guests needing towels should use guest towels.

As for the soaps, a qualified yes, do: If they are placed on or very near the sink, in a proximity that seems to invite their use; and if you may assume (short of asking to review your host's 1040 tax forms for the previous three years) that it would cause no financial hardship to replace them once they are used, then go ahead and scrub up. If, on the other hand, they are in a basket across the room, nestled among sprigs of lavender and baby's breath, assume their purpose is more decorative, and use the hunk of Ivory in the dish.

NOTE TO HOSTS: Some of you may be secretly grateful that guests are afraid to use these items, hoping—as with the mythical Christmas fruitcake, that gets re-gift-wrapped and presented year after year, from person to person, without ever actually being eaten— that a single set of towels and two or three pink soap scallop shells will last a lifetime. And, at the expense of your guests' comfort (and the state of your personal soaps and towels), they probably will.

For those who have gone to the trouble and expense of buying and displaying these things, and who only ask that they be used, teach via example. "Pre-use" them before the guests show up! Wash with, and leave in plain sight, a conspicuously defiled soap; then dry your inso- lent hands on a guest towel and "forget" to conceal it behind the others, for the world to gaze on in horror. The first guest to use the facility will think he or she is the second, will behold that the taboo (which no one can explain or really justify anyway) has been broken for all time (or at least the evening), and will feel free to break it, too.

But what about everything else in view and not nailed down? Once more, the ambiguity of the bathroom— public, or private?—makes visitors unsure as to **what**

they may and may not use. That hairbrush—may one appropriate it for a quick touch-up? And what about other grooming and cosmetological aids?

Soap and towels are, almost by definition, intended to be used by one and all. Other bathroom items, however, must be considered to be more personal in what is, after all, this most personal of all rooms. Therefore, refrain from borrowing, at least without asking first. Many sources said they wanted to be asked before guests helped themselves to perfume, hair spray, makeup, or feminine hygiene products, and one lady stated she keeps a supply of contact lens materials on hand specifically for company use only.

MI LOOFAH ES TU LOOFAH

You have stayed the night. Next morning, you are invited to use the shower. There, in the sanctity of the running water and concealment of the curtain or mottled glass, you discover an array of **shower items**: soaps, shampoos, "gels," back scrubbers, brushes, sponges, and other cleaning accessories that resemble either deep-sea creatures or oversized biscuits of shredded wheat. May you use them?

In general, yes. An exception might be made regarding smaller things you can only use once, like the one last sample-sized packet of shampoo on the counter, or the final bit of conditioner in a bottle. In either case, using it all up would be the equivalent of taking a person's last cigarette—a distinct and universally acknowledged manners crime back before smoking was suspect and smokers were objects of revulsion or pity.

Women are advised, however, not to cheat and move

the man's razor from the sink to the shower (if it isn't there to begin with), and then to "feel free" to use it on their legs. (If it *is* there to begin with, count to ten before growing suspicious that you may not be the only woman using the shower. Some men shave in the shower. Is there a small shaving mirror hanging off the shampoo caddy? Oh. Oh well . . .) Anyway, leg shaving with face razors is no minor offense: it dulls the blade, resulting in facial wear and, sometimes literally, tear for the hapless man who uses it next. Besides, in the area of personal grooming, men have too few opportunities to fetishize equipment and be finicky about their preferences. They will be quick to take advantage of the opportunity to act self-righteous and abused if they find you've misused their precious sixteen-cent disposable.

Of course, if you are in a position to take a shower at the home of another, you are probably on friendly, or intimate, enough terms to ask about certain items. Let's say—in fact, let's hope to God—you're given a towel. But you'd like a **washcloth**. (This is a deliberately inflammatory example. A small controversy seems to be raging, in the world of shower hygiene, over the utility and desirability of washcloths. One school holds that a shower just isn't adequate without one. The other condemns washcloths as playfields of bacteria. The relative merits of either position are, fortunately, none of *Mayflower Manners'* business.)

Assuming it is not a breach of public health to want a washcloth, the question arises: May you, in etiquette terms, request one?

Oh, why not. You're the guest, after all, and a person inviting you to take all your clothes off in a strange bathroom should be able to provide certain minimal creature comforts. Remember, though, that not all households stock washcloths.

As a guest, you owe it to your host to be considerate of him or her by not using all the **hot water**, being reasonable in your consumption of **shampoo**, etc., and leaving the place in at least as tidy a state as you found it with regard to **hair in the drain** (pick it out and discard), **towels** properly deployed on shower rod or towel rack (and not in a damp heap on the floor or, worse, on a bed, on a doorknob, or in a hamper), bits of shaved **beard in the sink** (rinse it all down), etc.

And speaking of towels, now is as good a time as any to issue **a few edicts about towels and bath mats**. Many women complain that they can never be sure of the cleanliness or the vintage of the towels they are handed, and feel better about the whole matter when they come fresh from the linen closet. (The towels, not the women.) As for rugs and bath mats, something clean ought to be underfoot (literally) when a guest steps from the shower: either a cleaned rug or, what is cheaper and easier to maintain, a bath mat. Be sure, in the latter case, not to leave it on the side of the tub while you shower, and to pick up the mat when you are finished with it, and hang it, spread out, where it may dry—the shower rod, for example. Abandoning it on the floor, to be trod on by everyone's shoes, is very bad form.

And if **the bathroom is so dirty** you just can't stand it? Can you, in order to bring yourself to use it, **clean parts of it yourself**? Yes, we're all appalled by such a notion, but no, it's not unheard of. Most of the women sources said they'd be horrified if a lover was so put off by their bathroom that he decided to take matters into his own hands. But some of the men (and women who don't clean their own places?) said they wouldn't mind. If you must clean, please do so as discreetly as possible.

No, this is not the most uplifting or romantic of subjects. Neither is the rest of this section. But then, that's the problem. With all our attention focussed on the uplifting and the romantic, it's easy to commit small gaffes, neglect irksome details, or take the fatally wrong, if tiny, thing for granted. Besides, as one source has said, "You can never be dished for being *too* clean."

RE PERSONAL HYGIENE

Consider, now, **the toothbrush**—the very symbol of staying the night. (When, in the movie *What's New, Pussycat?* bon vivant Peter O'Toole was asked by his secretary to sign a document, he produced from his jacket pocket a toothbrush and began, obliviously, trying to write his name. His character as a compulsive Casanova was encapsulated in that single prop: Here was a man who had more ready access to a toothbrush than a pen.) If your stay overnight at another's place was unpremeditated, you will—unless it's your habit to pack a kit of toiletries wherever you go—need a toothbrush the next morning.

What if you see only one—your host's—in the little holder? Should you use it? Hunt for another? Or is it permissible to ask for one? And, as long as you're looking around the bathroom for the essentials with which to start a new day, what about **deodorant**? May you use what's there?

First things first. We use the toothbrush from about

the age of three, when it is introduced to us as a sacred object of solemn bedtime ritual. And we keep using it, in larger but essentially unchanged versions, throughout our lives. Therefore we may find ourselves ascribing to it a significance left over from those days when brushing teeth was a major accomplishment, flossing was premature, and the departure of a tooth was a happy event, bringing money and praise (and a replacement tooth).

Not to be cynical, but by adulthood, the toothbrush isn't that big a deal any more. It is, after all, only a plastic stick with some nylon bristles at the end, and it costs about a dollar. So when the time comes that you need one, ask for it. Your host will probably have one or two spares—unused, of course, and still in the wrapper.

NOTE TO HOSTS: Do not respond to a request for a toothbrush by proudly producing a prettily decorated box stuffed with the things. Your guest will probably not appreciate being made to feel like just another in an endless stream of visitors, each presented with his or her own toothbrush like a child being rewarded by the doctor with a lollipop after braving a tetanus booster.

If, on the other hand, your host does not have a spare, smile and make noises to minimize the fuss and disappointment. Volunteer to go without, to use your finger, etc. And remember, next time, to pack your own. Remember, too, to stock them in your home—not only for intimate liaisons but for any houseguests who spend the night unexpectedly.

Do not, however, use your host's—at least, not without asking.

As for deodorant, clearly there is no harm in appropriating a can of spray. If, however, the product before you is a roll-on or a stick, you are advised to ask before using. If you find you're embarrassed to do so, take some consolation in the fact that your host will probably be embarrassed, too. That two adults can partake of sexual intimacy all night and then find the matter of sharing a toothbrush or a roll-on discomfiting is one of those things that people pretend to find fascinatingly ironic but, in truth, just don't want to talk about.

RE EVEN MORE PERSONAL HYGIENE

Some bathroom matters are universal but some are gender-specific. Of the latter, one of the more amusing (to men) and irksome (to women) is the business of leaving the **toilet seat** up. It is astounding how many men persist in committing this act of thoughtlessness. (It is also astounding how few women are willing to admit the humor in the slapstick consequences that can follow.) Still, funny or not, a man sharing a bathroom with a woman, even if (no, *especially* if) it is in his own home, should apply an ounce more common sense and devote a few more watts of attention, and put the seat down after he is finished. One of the hallmarks of being a good host, or a good guest, is not submitting your companion to unexpected cold baths, particularly at night when she is half asleep and has nothing more than a dim night-light by which to navigate.

So much for physical hazards. What about aesthetic ones? Meaning, inevitably, may a woman leave out in the open her **feminine hygiene products**? Or should she conceal them before entertaining?

Most men expressed little preference, except for douche

bags (meaning the items, not a category of men who were consulted), which they preferred not to have to confront. Women were split fifty-fifty. Still, surely caution dictates erring on the side of concealment. Proper etiquette involves not only the deferral of the personal in favor of the social, but also the pretense that there *is* no "personal." Consistent with this is the conceit that aside from possessing hands to shake, cheeks to kiss, and arms with which to give light, fond embraces, people don't really have bodies as such. Who, then, wants to stumble onto incontrovertible—and, to some, unappetizing—evidence to the contrary?

"But if we have an intimate relationship, isn't, as it were, the cat out of the bag? My boyfriend already knows I have a body . . ." Of course. But in that case, the consequence of keeping such products in sight is like that of a dictator inviting his guests to join him in a poolside frolic, while a dozen thug bodyguards stand around with machine guns. It has a certain chilling effect.

HOUSE DRESSING

In homes where there is no bathroom attached to the master bedroom, it is necessary to traverse a public space (the hall) en route to bath or shower. The stage is thus set for occasional moments of awkwardness (if not farce), when **employees** (babysitters, private nurses, housekeepers, etc.), circulating in the course of their daily routines, **encounter the towel- or robe-clad form of the man of the house** returning from bathroom to bedroom. Is there a dress, or rather, a half-dressed, code for such times? There is: Sources all thought that the man in question should wear a bathrobe, rather than a towel, in such circumstances—particularly in the presence of a teenage babysitter, whose most casual mention of a bare-chested father might cause understandable disquiet to her parents. But another source sensibly added that men wearing bath towels should not skulk or scurry, or in any other way act as though they were doing something wrong. Nor should they lean rakishly against a doorframe and engage whomever is passing by in casual banter, of course. Just go about your discreet, albeit half-naked, business.

Women, too, should wear robes when going to and from the bathroom. Even though most household work-ers, as mentioned above, are female, the babysitter's report of the lady of the house walking around naked or half-naked might spark rumors, begun by the girl's scan-dalized father, that your house is full of "nudists."

SUNDAY BLOODY SUNDAY

Women tempted to feel martyrish over all the time they spend in front of the mirror, preparing for work or play, should bear in mind that one thing they *don't* do is draw a finely honed steel blade across their throats every morn-ing, often causing pain and sometimes drawing blood. Probably most men will confess that the worst part of **cutting yourself shaving** is not the discomfort, but the inconvenience of staunching the flow. This is particularly true if you happen to be in someone else's home where, ironically, it is a bit more likely to happen than in your own. Why? Because, after an unplanned sleep-over, you confront the next morning without your usual equip-ment. She volunteers one of her razors. It's perfectly serviceable—but new, and therefore viciously sharp, and more likely to gouge and nick.

You do the best you can with water and tissues, but it often happens that in the course of a normal ablution, you get some red spots on the towel. And inevitably the towel is yellow, peach, pink, or some other pale, luscious, lovely pastel. Should you be sent to the guillotine?

No. You've suffered enough. It's one of those tragedies for which no one is to blame. Your hostess, however, should learn a lesson from it, i.e., to stock a supply of dark-colored towels for use by men who shave. It's either that, or put up with those tiny red speckles.

BOXED IN

Can't we find some other place to put the **cat box** besides the bathroom? The rationale for placing it there is obvious, of course, but it can also be argued that the bathroom is the one place we go in order to become clean. Now the kitchen is both the second most popular place, and even worse. If we had to choose between the two, the bathroom would get the reluctant nod, but still: Is there nowhere else? A closet, perhaps? The cat might object, and give you a look of recrimination, implying you consider her a second-class citizen of the household. But that's exactly what she is. She's a cat.

DATING

In General: **D**ating isn't what it used to be, but then, maybe it never was. In any case, for high school and college kids, the sexes are less polarized than in generations past, today's youth having grown up in times when girls have been allowed to be more "boylike" than before, and yes, boys to be more "girl-like." The result has been a lessening in the intensity of one-to-one couple relationships. Teens now date in groups, have many close friends of the opposite sex (with whom they will occasionally sleep), and generally shy away from the older "going steady" form of exclusivity.

People in their twenties do date in the traditional way, but apply distinctively untraditional criteria to their prospective partners. Especially in urban areas, women are likely to be concerned more with their careers than with simply "finding a man." And when they do find one, they want to see his tax forms, bank book, and pay stubs: mere romance is no longer sufficient for the generation of young career women raised to think that they can have it all.

Older people (age thirty to fifty) also date, but have by then usually been through at least one marriage. The women may have children; the men may have children. The women may have determined never to have them. The men, having not had them in their first marriage, may have determined to have them in their second.

All this transpires in an atmosphere in which sex has proven to be not the sin it was decreed, not the panacea it was once hoped, not the guilt-free recreation hinted at by psychology, not the liberating "energy" promised by New Age gurus, not the va-va-voom form of masculine self-expression explored ad nauseam in The Playboy Philosophy, not the touchy-feely Path to Personhood extolled by some feminist groups, not the Viable Lifestyle defended by gays. Sex, in the bad old days of repression, "making out," "copping a feel," and "scoring," was once an end in itself. In the crazy old days of "the sixties," it was a form of self-exploration. Today it is mainly a means, either of staving off loneliness, product testing for a mate, indulging in pleasure free of the dangers of drugs or cholesterol—or of acquiring a disease.

Sex is having an identity crisis. (For more, see "Sex," below.) Dating, which is to sex as training is to an athletic event, has changed accordingly. If you don't know whether you'll be running a mile or playing volleyball, your whole workout regimen goes up for grabs.

FEELED GOAL

Those dating, those thinking of dating, those having dated and withdrawn from the scene to take stock: All might well ask themselves, **What is the goal of dating these days?** What's the point of it all?

The one clear answer seems to be: Not just sex. This is worth stating because, a mere one generation ago, sex was the implicit goal of dating. The man agreed to provide companionship, entertainment, and food, and the woman agreed to "allow" him to go to bed with her. Or so the received notion went; that the man had as good a time going out as his partner, and the woman as good a time going to bed as her partner, was a fringe benefit. If the two fell in love, all the better.

Today, with sex both much more permissible and much more fraught with uncertainty, the goal of a date may be only secondarily to reach bed. Primarily it may be to enjoy companionship or reconnoiter for a mate. With this blurring of the line of division between the male and female roles on a date has come an easing of the tensions of etiquette. Before, when each had his or her specific role in the matter, the manners appropriate to each were sharply defined. Today everyone is responsible for everything. Good manners have less to do with chivalry than with common sense.

DATING THROUGH THE AGES

Where people are in life naturally affects the kind of dates they go on, and up to a certain age, where they are "in life" is the same as where they are in school. Thus, this **anatomy of a date**, as examined for four basic age groups:

HIGH SCHOOL: Boys and girls hang out in groups, go to movies, concerts, etc. in groups. It is perfectly appropriate for girls to ask out boys. It is during these group interactions that boys and girls size up prospective individual dates. A girl's (and, for that matter, a boy's) reputation still means something. In the one case, a girl will at any given time be sleeping with at most two boys, and will maintain a discreet silence about that fact. Boys, in contrast, will be sleeping with up to three or four different girls, and will bet their peers they can "bag" a specific girl. But even boys don't talk too much about their multiple partners.

The boy will pay all the expenses for the first few dates, after which rather than "going Dutch," the two will alternate picking up the whole tab for an evening. If he asks her to the prom—touchingly, everyone still goes—he will pay the usual expenses. If she asks him to her prom, she will pay for everything except his tuxedo and the corsage he still traditionally, poignantly gives her.

There is no set, understood number of dates prior to sex. Interestingly, while AIDS has captured the imagination of just about everyone, high school girls do not invariably carry condoms; sometimes those with steady boyfriends will, but mainly it's left to the boys.

The old-fashioned courtesies of holding doors, ordering in restaurants, etc. are dead as the dodo.

COLLEGE: Here, too, much socializing takes place in groups. Couples pair off at the end of the evening. Boys—or, as they are called in college, "men"—pay the lion's share of an evening's expense, with women ponying up for little things—popcorn at movies, a round of drinks at dinner, etc. Couples dining together regularly don't split checks, but take turns picking them up entirely.

The molecular structure of the college dating scene is larger scale than it once was: The one-on-one couple scene has yielded to these floating aggregations of individuals in larger groups. Most don't believe AIDS is a problem, but many—especially women—fear herpes. Condoms are used more often for birth control than for "safe sex." They are provided mainly by the men, although as always the savvy woman will keep them around, just in case.

Everyone has many friends of the opposite sex—a practice both suspiciously "queer" and unthinkably utopian to people who came of age in the 1950s. The women plan the group outings. One goes to a dance with a "date," but the term only signifies that that's the person with whom one is going to the dance. He (or she) could as likely be a buddy as a sexual partner.

POSTGRADS: People in their twenties, absorbed in the task of either starting or advancing their careers, have less time for group socializing. But the melody lingers on, so they congregate in groups of people their own sex, from which they make forays into dating individuals of the opposite. They will go Dutch, or alternate picking up the tab. Increasingly, a partner's social, professional, and financial bona fides become important (at least among people for whom such stuff matters). The strictures of "safe sex," like the Ten Commandments, are respected and in general obeyed. But the overriding fear is of herpes and other sexually transmitted diseases besides AIDS. By now women have condoms in their homes.

Women also become aware of their biological clocks. Men become aware of women's biological clocks when, as happens increasingly as the woman nears thirty, the subjects of marriage and children arise. The chief obstacle to love and romance, however, is work: A woman can be as avid a careerist as any man and, between her job, physical fitness, hanging out with friends, and pursuing her lifestyle (cooking, travel, decorating her home, etc.), can find that there aren't enough hours in the day to fill in, in one's Filofax, all the things one has to do.

Men continue to congregate in groups, often for the purpose of drinking.

Sex is no longer the chummy, between-friends thing it was in college. As childbearing deadlines loom, and with the natural maturation of the personalities of people nearing thirty, dates start to lead toward serious relationships. A first date rarely leads to bed, but because everyone's schedule is so darn busy, it may not be much later than the second or third. That at least some of this hyperkinetic lifestyle, with its fifty-or-more-hour work-week, may be a way of avoiding sex, and its concomitant possible problems, is something only the very confident, or the very simpleminded, will deny.

AGING BABY BOOMERS: Among people age thirty-three or over, the older verities apply. The men ask the women on dates, though only after the woman has made it unambiguously clear that she'd be interested. Cooking, of all things, becomes a key indicator for men. Actually, it makes sense: If a man lives alone, he is unlikely to cook much, and one can grow weary of restaurant food, restaurant rules, restaurant public display. If, by around the third date, she neither asks him out to eat nor offers to cook for him, he will take it as a sign that she's not interested—or, not up to snuff. Said one source, "Men resent women who don't cook."

There is no set number of dates before sex. AIDS haunts the scene, and even men don't want to sleep with someone after only one date. What a source referred to as "the hysteria over condoms" seems to have dissipated—at least among men, who use them more for birth control than disease prevention. By his mid-thirties, many a man has either first- or secondhand experience (a friend) with paternity suits.

Women, however, use and stock condoms to prevent herpes, etc. People from certain professions are thought to be worse herpes risks than others: modeling, music, entertainment. AIDS per se is not discussed much, and most women are not actually worried about their dates having been bisexual. However, one source reported a woman who routinely sent her prospective lovers to her doctor to be tested. Yes, she paid for it. (If that isn't a pure example of *Mayflower Manners*, nothing is.)

Some men perform some of the old-fashioned courtesies: While almost no one orders for women in restaurants, most men are conscientious about walking on the curb side of the sidewalk.

Dates now don't lead particularly to marriage (they may be leading away from previous marriages), but there is less sex than there used to be. The one-night stand is seen as a form of Russian roulette.

What do men want? A little of everything: many men will not go out with women who do not work, but they will also look askance at women so involved in their careers as not to have time to devote to them. Some women (a source estimates them at 30 to 40 percent of the total) are indeed looking for a husband whose income will allow them not to work. Many more women than ever before do not want to have children.

TIPS FOR TEENS

With "going out" such a miasma of unclear rules, are there any **pointers** the aspiring dater can learn, and still be confident they will apply in whatever context he or she finds himself or herself in? No. But here are a few rules of thumb:

In the city, first dates can often take place at a fancy restaurant; in the suburbs, a more casual venue is appropriate. Everyone, everywhere, should avoid the most expensive places. And women ordering from the menu, free to tell the waiter themselves what they want, should decline to order the most expensive thing.

Often the man will not want to decide where to go, and will ask the woman to choose. She should ask him the kinds of foods he likes, then present him with a selection of three or four places, covering a range of cuisines and prices. As one source said of men, "They want you to decide, but they also want a choice."

Women with drastically restricted diets—i.e., women who "don't eat anything"—annoy men. If a woman's diet is so restrictive—no meat, no dairy, no this, no that—she should mention it, promote something else as the main activity of the date, and relegate eating to a secondary function.

It is appropriate for a man to pick up a woman for the first couple of dates. Later, if all is going well, he may ask her to meet him at a particular place.

AIDS BEFORE BEAUTY

For probably most heterosexuals, AIDS is more a symbol of "dangerous sex," or irresponsibility, than a felt threat. (Homosexuals do not enjoy that luxury.) Still, the question arises: **How does one talk about AIDS with a prospective partner?**

One begins with the assumption that the partner knows about it. It is not seemly, nor necessary, to smile on the first date and say, "Love your dress. By the way, will you be giving me a fatal disease?" The subject is both too delicate, and too statistically remote, to merit such direct confrontation. Instead, allow time to pass—that's what these dates are for, after all—during which you get acquainted with the sort of person with whom you're dealing. By the time sex itself seems a possibility, you will have necessarily both crossed that line beyond which these sensitive issues may be discussed. Note, too, that most straights are more worried about other maladies than about AIDS.

When the time comes, be circumspect but not too vague. Don't say, "I have my doubts as to whether you're a safe person to sleep with." Instead, say, "I'm a little worried about you-know-what . . . have you been tested?" Of course it will not do to ask such a thing if you yourself have not been tested.

And if your partner says no, that he or she has not been tested?

Then you have a decision to make. You may, without violating any code of manners, say something like "Then we'd better cool it until you are, if you don't mind. I'd just feel better that way." As in other examples of coaxing another to behave a certain way, place the blame for the request on yourself.

What if he says yes, and you don't believe him?

Then again, you have a decision to make. Why don't you believe your partner? If it's because you think him or her capable of lying about such a thing, then you are either growing paranoid or are dating someone with whom perhaps you had better *not* have a sexual relationship. In response to his reply you may, if you still harbor doubts, either be sure to use a condom and take your chances (they are remote that you will be infected), or beg off, blaming yourself with a comment such as "I'm sorry, I don't think I'm ready for this yet. I guess I'm just too worried about it."

All of this applies to herpes and other sexually transmitted diseases, too. Sexual virtue has given way to health virtue, and as with any virtue, it's difficult to offer conclusive proof. Note that one of the more sinister things about AIDS is that while A and B may trust their previous lovers (C and D) were safe, C and D may not be able to feel the same about *their* previous lovers. Somewhere in the endless family tree of who has slept with whom, uncertainty can enter: The most elaborate and credible network of trust and respect among sexual partners can break when one member of the grid sleeps with another whose past is not what it should have been. Whose "fault" it is becomes moot, and in any case is difficult to trace.

All this can be dispelled conclusively with a lab test. If that is what it takes to make you comfortable, you will have to say so in a nonjudgmental, nonaccusatory way. Short of that, everything devolves on trust.

FULL DISCLOSURE

People with AIDS are mostly gay, users of intravenous drugs, or sexual partners of IV drug-users. **If a host invites a known carrier of the disease to a dinner party, should he so inform his other guests?**

Yes. Most people will know that they cannot contract the disease by being seated at a dinner table with a carrier. But it is a courtesy to all to let them know ahead of time.

And if the carrier offers you something that makes you wary—a sip of wine from his glass, say—how should you react?

Well, he won't. People who know they have AIDS are literally painfully aware of what they can and can't do as regards the rest of the population. If you are unsure how to react to such an offer, decline it as you would anything else you don't care to try.

DATING AND OTHER SERVICES

In General: Using an intermediary to facilitate romance seems . . . well, unromantic. Indeed, part of the bliss of true love is the fact of two people having met at all—having "found each other" in spite of the bigness and badness of the big bad world. If we have to hunt for romance, and recruit third parties to provide the object of our desire, it seems artificial, or cheating, like going to a nursery where they systematically cultivate four-leaf clovers, "finding" one, and then wondering why we don't get good luck.

But then, sometimes people aren't looking for romance, true love, or good luck. They want *a date*. And intermediaries, whether a friend arranging a blind date or an agency with a questionnaire and a list, start to seem like a sensible source. The etiquette of such occasions resembles that for an ordinary date—with suitable attention given, of course, to the somewhat contrived nature of its arrangement.

ENLISTING IN THE SERVICE

Having acknowledged that happenstance, luck, and your job aren't doing your social life any favors, you decide to call a "**dating service**"—which sounds coolly professional, but which, now that you think of it, might just turn out to be an old-fashioned matchmaker with delusions of grandeur and a computer. Will things start getting Old World on you? Or **will the etiquette you know prove to be sufficient?**

Relax. Whether you're matched up with Mr. Right or Mr. Rogers, Ms. Right or Ms. Havisham, your standard date-smarts will stand you in good stead. Commit these self-evident tips to memory:

BASIC ETIQUETTE FOR THE ARRANGED DATE

*(Note: Many of the following also apply to **the blind date**.)*

1. Start with Sunday brunch. Yes, it's corny, and no, it's not as romantic as a "drink" or "dinner," but then, that's the point. This first encounter is not really a date, but an audition. For both of you.

2. Let not either party pick up the other at his/her dwelling. Meet at the venue. Those who have to ask why should be even more certain to follow this rule than those who don't. Oh, all right: because, despite your intermediary's best intentions, your gentleman caller could in the event prove to be a "weirdo." Better to discover this in a public place than on your doorstep. Actually, you could be a weirdo, too.

3. The man may choose the place, but should not be pushy about it.

4. The lady should offer to split the cost of the meal, but the man should be prepared to pick up the tab. Play it by ear; some men are offended if a lady offers to pay her share, some if she doesn't.

5. She should not order the most expensive thing on the menu. Unless he does.

6. If your meeting has been arranged by a dating service, DO NOT discuss the service, the other dates it's arranged for you, your increasing skepticism that it'll ever find someone "half decent" for you, etc. Nor should you discuss past relationships, divorces, disasters, your own inability to relate to the opposite sex, ad nauseam.

In fact, neither of you should acknowledge explicitly that you've met via a paid intermediary. If you must allude to the third party, try to do so as though mentioning a friend. The less self-conscious you both are about the mercenary (in the professional sense) basis of your encounter, the better.

7. If all seems to be going swimmingly, it is perfectly appropriate for her to ask him to an event in the near future.

8. He should (if they live in a city and it's necessary) put her in a cab. He need not offer to pay her fare.

9. Afterwards, call the service and report in about how it "went." Proprietors of such services are professionally, and often personally, anxious to know. They want their clients to be satisfied, presumably trusting that while your happiness may make it unnecessary for you to purchase their services in the future, your enthusiastic recommendation of them to your friends will compensate for their loss of you as a customer.

10. If it doesn't work out, use the service as a buffer. A man may ask the service to convey duly euphemized regrets; a woman may ask it to tell the man that a previous date (introduced by the service) has resurfaced in her life. True, in all this it is assumed that the man is the more aggressive and active of the pair. If that offends

you, simply arrange with the service to convey an excuse of which you approve.

11. If it continues to work out well, let the proprietors of the service know. Not only will they be pleased, but you will spare them the wasted effort of lining up other dates for you, and from misleading other clients.

12. Play fair with the service. If you go zero-for-five with the dates it arranges, ask yourself whether you've given it a true description of who you are and what you are looking for. Many clients, when asked to describe themselves upon signing with a service, wax eloquent about—it turns out—who they want to be, who they plan to be, etc.

And be sure to reveal all the relevant facts: One source mentioned a woman who was fixed up with a man who collected wine. Only then did she inform all concerned that she was a member of Alcoholics Anonymous. Withholding such relevant truths from your dating service can be worse than withholding them from your attorney. In the latter case, you can go to jail. In the former, you can find yourself on a date of a sort to make you long for solitary confinement.

And don't try to gouge the service for one more referral, with the claim that this one "didn't count" or that one was "their fault." The service is just that—a professional agency. As with every other professional organization, you pays your money and you takes your chances.

As for **blind dates**, because the intermediary is a mutual friend, relative, or acquaintance, that person becomes a perfectly appropriate topic for preliminary conversation. And, of course, it is not necessary to phone the intermediary the next day to "report in." Otherwise, though, the above suggestions hold, with the unfortunate addendum that an intermediary who fixes two people up for a blind date is less responsible if it misfires than an agency. Such an individual is simply indulging in a bit of free-lance matchmaking; an agency is charging good money.

IT IS A ROLL OF MONEY IN MY POCKET, AND I AM HAPPY TO SEE YOU

Speaking of good money: For those for whom a dating service is too long-range, and indeed for whom a "date" must be arranged immediately, and on very clear terms, there is the **escort service**. *Mayflower Manners* knows that you know that it knows that you know that this controversial topic is one with which it has some familiarity. For the benefit of those readers who don't know what all this winking is about, however, this introductory summary of what an escort service is and does:

An escort service provides female companionship on an hourly basis, for an hourly fee. "Companionship" in this sense means everything from companionship to everything. Usually the client is interested mainly, if not exclusively, in sexual favors, but not always. Sometimes he wants companionship *and* sexual favors, in which case he takes his escort out to dinner, say, prior to returning with her to the home or hotel, at which point the next phase of the evening begins. Sometimes he just wants someone attractive to talk to. In any case, after the customer is finished, the woman leaves.

"True love" it isn't—but then, that's not what either

party is seeking. Accordingly, dealing with an escort service is a bit more cut-and-dried than with a dating service.

BASIC ETIQUETTE FOR ARRANGED SEX
(How to Deal with an Escort Service)

1. Decide exactly what sort of "escorting" you want. There are agencies that cater to the desire for a brief, strictly physical encounter; and there are those, charging between $150 and $200 an hour, which offer a more refined experience. (What follows applies to dealing with the latter.)

2. After calling, when inquiring as to which young ladies are available for that evening, don't ask crudely, "Whaddaya got tonight?" Instead, tell whoever answers the phone your name and where you are, and wait to be asked what kind of young lady you would like to see. If you aren't asked, assume you are dealing with a service which will provide you with a warm body and not much more. Clients interested in companionship as well as sex are advised to deal with an agency that takes the trouble to learn what the customer wants.

3. And you may indeed tell the agency what you want. But there is no need to be vulgar: Of the many colorful ways there are of saying, for example, "large breasts," choose the most discreet ("generously endowed"), and don't bother worrying whether you will be understood. The person on the other end of the line has such conversations, and bandies such terms, every night. And then some.

4. NEVER MENTION SEX. Don't ask for it, don't

ask if it's included in the hourly fee. (If you do, you will be met with either a bland, mystifying denial, or a click and a dead phone line.) If you want to know if sex is included in the quoted fee, ask, "Is tipping involved?" If it is—if the fee quoted is called an "introduction fee" or an "agency fee"—then sex is extra, and you will have to negotiate what, and how much, with the young lady when she calls you back. If it is not involved, the fee covers sex, too.

5. After reaching an agreement with the agency, you will hang up. Soon, the young lady will call. It is then that you may discuss with her any special activities you may fancy. She will be more open in her discussion than the agency was, but still: Be discreet.

6. Because you are dealing with an escort service, your escort will come to you, whether you intend her to escort you on a night on the town or to a chair across the room. It is polite for you to take her coat, if she has one. It will be polite (as well as professionally responsible) of her to be on time. Amazing as it may seem to some readers, it is *not* considered polite for the man to pounce upon the woman immediately after she enters the room. It is considered thoughtful to offer her a drink—if not at, say, the hotel bar, then via room service, or from your own supply. Be sure to order ahead of her arrival, unless the prospect of waiting for a tardy bottle of champagne, while her meter is running, appeals to you.

7. Most services ask for payment up front, after receipt of which many employees are required to phone their offices and report in. Don't take it personally. She, meanwhile, should be discreet about it, murmuring, "Yes,

everything is fine," into the phone rather than barking, "Yeah, I got the bread."

8. During drinks—note that often agencies only permit their employees to drink wine, champagne, or soft drinks—it is good manners to chat. Later, when the mood is more relaxed and some rapport has been established—*then* may one pounce? Assuredly not. Then one may suggest that the two of you "get a little closer," or "get more comfortable."

9. It is not polite to take advantage of the young lady, to demand more than was originally agreed on (in terms of activities). If you want her to stay longer than was planned, acknowledge that the hourly fee remains in effect, and let her check her office.

Do not try to coax from her her real name, or her phone number—or, for that matter, her social security number or her mother's maiden name. Do not try to cadge a few more minutes when she says she must leave. She, on the other hand, should not leave simply because you have finished before the allotted time whatever you wanted to do.

And do not claim, after letting her stay two hours when one was agreed on, that she remained the additional hour because she liked you so much. Sound absurd? It happens all the time.

IT PREYS TO ADVERTISE
Another way of meeting and being met is via **the personals column of a newspaper or magazine**. Here the model is not so much matchmaking as job hunting. If Sandy places an ad, and Randy replies with a letter, and

Sandy is intrigued enough to arrange a meeting, who is the "host"?

The dynamics of the situation would suggest Sandy; it was she, after all, who "created" the position and advertised its availability, and she who screened the respondents and selected Randy. She's the "boss" in this increasingly inadequate metaphor.

But it would be better manners for neither to assume that role. Both should instead strive for mutuality. Randy, rather than entering into the relationship like an underling who has pleased a prospective employer, should bear in mind that in a sense *he* "approved" *her*, that her personals ad was as much a Situation Wanted as a Help Wanted, and her description of herself therein a sort of mini-resume. Might it be a good idea for each of them to regard their meeting as one in which two peers have exchanged resumes, and have agreed to hire each other? Maybe not. Still, you get the idea.

Bad form: showing letters and photos of respondents to friends.

$\mathcal{S}$EX

In General: **I**s there such a thing as "sexual etiquette"? Should there be? Can there be?

Not every etiquette authority seems to think so. In fact, *no* other etiquette authority seems to think so: None of the major arbiters of etiquette (they know who they are, and so do you) offer much advice about the do's and don'ts, the totems and taboos, the "May we?" and "Mai, oui" of sex. At best, one gets arch commentary about how such matters are none of etiquette's (otherwise inexhaustible) business; at worst, dutiful commonsensical remarks about . . . oh, you know—*courtship*.

Mayflower Manners believes there is, should, and can be such a thing as sexual etiquette, because sex has become both less important and more important than it used to be. Less important, because, from the time of the arrival of the illustrious ship from which *Mayflower Manners* derives its catchy alliterative name, sex has become decreasingly *sinful*. Nathaniel Hawthorne's Hester Prynne may have been branded as an outcast and compelled to wear the stigmatizing *A* for adultery in Colonial times, but today she would be just another "unwed mother," sporting (if she could afford to) a conspicuously displayed *A* for Armani.

Sin has been bred out of sex like the strings that no longer have to be pulled off green beans. As a result sex is less personal—paradoxically, less intimate—than it used to be. Morally, sex is "okay," and therefore, inevitably, more mundane. When it was either a sacrament of marriage or a sin against God, it was either above or beneath etiquette, too personal or too evil to be subject to good manners. Now it's just another form of intercourse, and as such requires a code of manners like any other social activity.

But sex is also more important than it used to be. Ever since Freud, science—and, therefore, society—has viewed sex as a sort of laboratory for investigating and improving one's psychological "health." Not only is sex morally "okay," it's psychologically important. "You *may* Do It" has gradually become "You *should* Do It." (This has particularly applied to women who, between feminism and the advent of The Pill, have been the recipients of both permission and pressure to have more sex.)

The threat of AIDS, herpes, and other sexually transmitted diseases, of course, has had a dampening effect on the wild and crazy sexuality of the sixties and seventies, but the postwar (World War II), post-Pill ethos persists: People have many sexual partners whom they are not in love with, engaged to, married to, or even on a first-name basis with. That's where etiquette steps in, after knocking politely. It all comes down to a simple three-step formula:

1. Etiquette exists to guide the interactions of strangers and acquaintances.

2. People have sex with strangers and acquaintances.

3. People need—and willy-nilly practice—sexual etiquette.

This being the case, why not say so? The mere presence of another person, no matter how mundane the context—at a bus stop, on a plane, at a lunch counter, in a bank line—invokes etiquette, makes it relevant, brings it into play. Mutual expectations arise. Each party becomes conscious of his or her "rights," and obligations, vis-à-vis the other. There is no need to be polite when you are alone; the word is meaningless. But there is every need to be so when someone else shows up.

How much more true this is when someone else shows up, takes off his or her clothes, and starts Doing It. Properly addressing a bar mitzvah invitation to the chargé d'affaires of the Venezuelan consulate is all well and good; but isn't it in bed that you *really* want to do the right thing?

PASSES ATTEMPTED, PASSES COMPLETED
It may be many things, but **is it rude to make a pass?** Should one feel rebuked if turned down?

(Granted, "make a pass" sounds slightly antique. But "proposition" sounds pushy. Worse, it's a noun swaggering around as a verb, and reminds one of those slightly scary transformations by which "disappear," a formerly charming intransitive verb ["The magician made the bunny disappear"] becomes a sinister transitive verb ["Suspecting him of leftist sympathies, the Buenos Aires secret police disappeared the magician"]. Besides, "making a pass" has a thrilling World War II aerial dogfight connotation, suggesting fighter planes swooping down with guns blazing. So let's use that.)

Meaning: One can decline the offer, but is it insulting even to be asked? Or is it *pretend* insulting, ostensibly insulting, i.e., insulting unless the person asked says yes, in which case its character as an insult is retroactively erased? (This sort of thing was common in 1950s Hollywood movies: Kirk Douglas makes a pass at Susan

Hayward. She is "insulted," and slaps him. He laughs, kisses her. She kisses back. He picks her up and carries her into the bedroom. She does not resist. It's not insulting anymore.)

Let us say, truthfully but unhelpfully, that it all depends on technique. A rude pass is rude; a tactful one is not. Note here that "making a pass" is different from "seduction." The former consists in proposing sex per se; the latter, in leading up to proposing (or initiating) sex via proposing other, ostensibly "innocent," activities (e.g., "Let's have a drink," "Let's listen to some music," "Gee, it's warm in here. Let's you take your clothes off," etc.).

A pass is neither inherently good nor bad. If made with sensitivity, it is at worst flattering, at best welcome. But if made brusquely, crudely, or prematurely, it can suggest that the "receiver" (who else is a pass intended for, if not a receiver?) is undiscriminating about her (or his) sexual partners—is, in another term not much heard these days, "easy." *That* is what's insulting: not the offer itself, but the offer made under those circumstances.

There is also the inappropriate pass, which most commonly occurs when either or both of the concerned parties are married. (There are other examples, of course: when the parties are blood relatives, members of different species, etc.) The ethics of the matter aside, the pass reveals the passer's good or bad manners by how obviously the receiver has indicated his or her marital status. That is, the etiquette of the pass is about how it's done, not whether it's done.

For example, if at a party, Billy and Billie are chatting, and Billie makes significant mention of her husband ("Oh dear, I think my husband's had one too many. He's juggling the steak knives again . . ."), it is impolite for Billy to make a pass. At least, technically. It is not impolite for him to say, e.g., "How embarrassing for you. Why don't we go to my place and talk about it?" But then, for that, see above re "seduction." Eventually in this process—and *Mayflower Manners* can hardly believe it is saying this—etiquette becomes secondary to getting on with things.

As for being turned down, it needn't necessarily be a rebuke. "No" doesn't always mean "—and how dare you ask." (It may not even mean "—and that's final," but merely "no, for now.") Of course, if the pass has been impolite, the rejection may well be harsh. Unfortunately, one can make the most well-intentioned, tactfully executed pass in the world, and still be refused with self-righteous indignation. As in every other kind of exchange, displaying good manners toward someone brings no guarantee that they will be reciprocated.

FLIRTATION DEVICES

Making a pass is the amorous equivalent of "calling" in poker, a formal invitation to put up or shut up. But what about preliminary stages? **Is there, for example, an etiquette to flirting?**

Of course. Actually, the etiquette of flirting and the technique of flirting are almost indistinguishable. Flirting should above all be light and casual, and never acknowledge itself. Flirtation starts off as impersonal, or fake-personal (via teasing and mock insults), and only progresses to the truly personal with both partners' consent. As with making a pass, both parties are obliged to inform each other of the existence of spouses, boy/girlfriends, etc. This issuing of fair warning should be tactful, lest the possible purpose of the flirting be prematurely revealed, causing what is known in polite circles as an "awkward moment."

Flirting can be an end in itself, and would-be flirts are cautioned not to impute too much meaning to a partner's words and manner. It is not bad manners to flirt for hours, and then refuse to take it any further. But it is disingenuous to pretend not to know that much flirting does, in fact, lead to more physical forms of expression. It's important, therefore, to try to gauge a person's ultimate intentions, lest you say or do something inappropriately leading.

Fortunately, it has sometimes been possible to read people's ultimate intentions in the way they conform to certain basic sexual stereotypes. Unfortunately, all that is out the window. The characteristic roles of men and women for flirtation have been hopelessly jumbled: Most women born before 1960 will usually expect men to take the lead, while those born after 1960, and especially in the seventies, will be comfortable with a more aggressive posture. Most men born before 1955 will adopt a relatively aggressive stance, while those born after (and especially in the seventies) will be more accustomed to aggressive women, and not assume—as would older men—that a woman who takes the initiative is looking for some quick action.

It is tempting, in this day and age, to regard flirtation as a sort of negotiation toward some sexual "deal." It is also indescribably vulgar. Rather, think of flirtation as an improvised playlet, the climax of which remains a mystery until it is reached. Etiquette, in such circumstances, consists in being generous and sensitive to your fellow actor.

Speaking of your fellow actor, several sources took pains to note that a woman, when flirting, should respect the "turf" of another woman, i.e., should not pursue the other woman's partner without first asking about the nature of their relationship and allowing the turf-guarding woman the opportunity to voluntarily step aside. This is a combination of ethics (forbidding poaching on another's preserve . . .) and etiquette (. . . without asking permission), and as such is a quite charming way to address a nasty, cutthroat issue.

CONDOM MINIMUMS

But enough of the preliminaries. You've met, flirted, made passes, and received them. All has gone swimmingly, but there is the matter of protection. The reference is not to paying off the Mafia so they don't firebomb your dry cleaning shop. The reference is to **condoms. Is it assumed that the man will provide them? Is it therefore rude of the woman to preempt that sacred responsibility by producing them herself?**

Nothing is assumed—or, rather, it is assumed only that someone had better come up with one. If the woman produces them before the man, he should not feel as though his manly duty has been usurped. He should instead feel thankful that she is being sensible. (If he's neglected to provide them, he should feel secretly relieved that she's taken him off the hook.)

As for actually using condoms, if two people agree not to, that is their prerogative; that choice may be any one of several things, but it is not a breach of etiquette. Any disagreement over condoms, however, should be resolved in favor of their use—not because it is the safer option (it is, but that's a matter of science, not etiquette), but because sometimes good manners consist of putting the other person at ease. The annoyance the man might feel at being forced to wear a condom is as nothing compared to the fear the woman might feel were he not to wear one.

This holds, therefore, **even if the man is sure he is not infected with the HIV virus—in fact, even if he has been recently tested for it**. If she insists, he should wear it. This may sound a bit dogmatic, if not actually hysterical. But think of how she feels. Unless he can present an official document attesting to his virus-free status, how can she know he is "safe"? Because he says so, and she should trust him? In a relationship of some standing, maybe. But with someone she's known for two weeks?

Men for whom this argument only serves to increase an already huffy mood should pause a moment and reflect that condom protection works both ways. Wearing one protects him, too. After all, how does he know *she's* "safe"? Has she been tested?

For her part, a woman who overrides her lover's objections about wearing a condom should do what she can to help him enjoy the experience. She could incorporate its manipulation (no, not that; the manipulation of the *condom*) into their lovemaking, and generally help take the onus of awkwardness, silliness, and implicit danger off its use.

YES, IT SO HAPPENS THAT I DO TALK TO MY MOTHER WITH THIS MOUTH

One of the differences between alcoholic intoxication and sexual arousal is that being drunk makes you say wild things you don't mean, while being sexually turned on makes you say wild things you *do* mean. Rather, you mean them at the moment; afterwards, and during daily, unaroused life, you not only don't mean them, but you would hardly dare say them. In fact it would take a concerted mental effort even to think of them. After some concentration, several examples will come to mind, and *Mayflower Manners* will thank you to keep them to yourself.

But while we might like to think we "can say anything" during sex, still the question occurs: **Can we say *anything?*** No matter how dirty, violent, degrading, cruel, or weird? Is sex, in this sense, a sort of sanctioned sadism (or insanity), permitting us to say whatever comes to mind, safe in the understanding that afterward we'll agree it "never happened"? **Or is it possible to go Too Far?**

Both. First-time partners should feel free, as they say, to "experiment," but only on the understanding that what to them is titillatingly raw and satisfyingly carnal may be, to their partner, a complete gross-out. If it is, the partner should feel free—should be made to feel free—to say so in subsequent, less hectic moments.

Meanwhile, the partner should bear in mind that what appeals to the talker is, usually, the *expression* of the raunchy sentiments to which he or she is giving voice. That is, it's a turn-on to say such things, without (a) meaning them literally, (b) meaning them personally, (c) proposing that either or both partners actually do them, (d) with or, (e) to, each other. The recipient of such comments should therefore not take offense at anything said, no matter how offensive.

As for saying "please" and "thank you" in the heat of passion, *Mayflower Manners* will waive that requirement.

WILL YOU, WON'T YOU, WOULD YOU, COULD YOU . . . UH . . .

Naturally, all our lovemaking is perfectly spontaneous and inspired, a flawlessly synchronized pas de deux in which each partner knows intuitively which actions and maneuvers will please the other and, not coincidentally, how to go about them. It remains only to add that the preceding sentence is a pathetic lie.

In fact, when it comes to sex, we may not know much about physiology, but we know what we like. Sadly, the other person may know a great deal about physiology but, usually, doesn't know what we like. And vice versa. **Is there a proper way to ask the partner to do X, or Y, or even (what the hell) Z? And is there an equally proper way to decline?**

There is, and there is, and both have in common the central premise of good manners, viz., consideration for the other person's feelings. Self-evident? Not during sex it isn't, immersed as we are in consideration of our own feelings, and touchings, and so forth.

Start, then, with the assumption that your partner is truly interested in making you happy and giving you pleasure. (If you can't assume that, you're in for a peculiar time in bed, and manners, Mayflower or otherwise, can't help you.) Follow with the understanding that most partners will be thrilled to be told what you like, what "works." Wouldn't you? So ask—not formally, as one would say, "Please pass the salt" (unless you like salt in bed), but with the amatory equivalent: "I just love it when you [etc.]" or "One of the things I like the most is [etc.]" or "If you really want to make me crazy, try [etc.]"

"But wait a minute," someone will say. "They don't talk that way in Harold Robbins, Eric van Lustbader, and other books in which people have fabulous sex. They say things like, 'TOUCH ME THERE! NOW! WITH YOUR FOOT! OR I'LL KILL YOU!' Isn't that the proper way for hot, with-it, sexed-up moderns to talk in bed?"

No. This is not trash fiction, where one-dimensional characters couple and claw at each other with snarls and gasps like battling dinosaurs. This is your life. It's also the life of your partner. For saying extreme things out loud for the sheer dirty fun of it, see the section above. For requesting that another party do you a service or a favor, the pivotal concept is that of requesting, not demanding.

And, having requested and been granted your heart's, or whatever is the operative organ's, desire, do your partner **the courtesy of responding.** Verbally, audibly, so he/she knows they're doing the right thing. If you don't, your partner will assume he/she's doing the wrong thing, and either struggle on in an ever-escalating spiral of ludicrously varied technique, or stop altogether. The former turns sex into smutty slapstick, while the latter prompts people to bark commands ("Don't stop!") like a character in Harold Robbins.

But of course, there are requests, and there are *requests*. What if you're on the receiving end of one of the latter, that is, what if you don't want to do the thing requested? **How do you (as the First Lady said to the drug addict) "just say no"?**

The answer is, via a two-step process. Step One consists in diversionary misdirection: Indicate "not just now" and proceed, a bit aggressively, to do something to/for your partner you know he/she likes. Or redirect your partner's actions by saying, "Oh, but I love it when you [etc.] so much . . . ," and try to transform yourself from the request receiver to the requester per se.

Step Two, while not as immediately implemented, is nonetheless important to minimize strain in your relationship. Afterward, perhaps in that warm, contented glow that comes when two people lie in each other's arms following a mutually satisfying round of lovemaking— or, if one partner falls asleep, perhaps on a crosstown bus the next day—discuss what has transpired. Voluntarily acknowledge that you indeed didn't really want to do X. But take pains to avoid being judgmental, either morally or esthetically. Blame yourself. "I don't think that's something I'd be comfortable with right now" is one way to apologize, as is "I guess I must be different than most people. I've never really enjoyed that." Make it your problem, not your partner's.

THE ANSWER, MY FRIEND . . .

It's time for *Mayflower Manners* to take the opera gloves off and get down to cases. All this shilly-shallying about is-there-sexual-etiquette and isn't-sex-too-private-to-be-subject-to-manners vanishes like the morning mist in the presence of the subject of fellatio. The reader knows what's being alluded to here (unless, that is, the reader is a girl or boy in her or his early teens, paging through this book while babysitting for a neighbor, hoping to find the dirty parts and instead getting only advice about how to be polite).

Yes, *that*. And now every reader knows what's coming next, i.e., the matter of—well, there seems to be no way to avoid actually saying it—**swallowing**.

If ever a single phenomenon proved the need for—and indeed, the de facto existence of—sexual etiquette, it's this. It is an activity which some women enjoy, and others abhor; men, meanwhile, seem to fetishize it precisely to the extent that women find it abhorrent. "If she really loved me, she'd do it" goes the prevailing attitude, which somehow omits its corollary, "If he really loved me, he wouldn't ask me to do it."

But enough temporizing. **What's the good manners position on swallowing?**

That it is optional. Unless a man knows that his partner is partial to such behavior, he should let her know when he is about to climax, to give her the opportunity to conclude things with her hand. Or, at an earlier point in the activity, he can ask her (see above) if she minds. But he should respect her decision regardless, and not fall into the (slightly childish) assumption that her willingness or lack thereof is somehow proof of her "real" feelings for him. Some women just don't like it, no matter how they feel about their lovers.

And another thing. It has come to *Mayflower Manners'*

attention that some women find themselves in the situation just discussed after their partner has literally **forced their heads down** to where they want them to be. This—need it be said?—will never do. A bit of encouragement, a nonverbal cue, a light touch of her head in the proper direction—fine. But brute placement of the partner's head, as though positioning a sculptural model or practicing chiropractic neck manipulations, is most rude. As one source put it, women will "go down there when they're damn good and ready," and "feeling pressured will only add to their distaste and dislike for that activity."

While we're on, or rather, near, the subject, we might wonder, on behalf of men, **whether it's bad manners for a woman to refuse to perform oral sex at all**. The answer is a slightly qualified no. It's always appropriate to decline to do something you don't wish to do. And while what passes for "standard activity" varies from person to person, it is not inconceivable that a majority of women readers find themselves in bed with people for whom oral sex is, at least as a preliminary stage of things, normal and assumed. Consequently, while a woman may with impunity decline to do it once or twice or three times, by the fourth or fifth time her partner might consider her refusal a "problem," as in the catchall rhetorical (yet deeply felt) query, "What's your problem?"

And while it is not bad manners to reply that you just don't care for that sort of thing, that will not keep your partner from wondering why not, and hoping you'll change your mind. How long you will be able to "get away" with such a policy will vary from partner to partner.

IT'S THE TIME OF THE MONTH FOR MY FRIEND TO VISIT AND FALL OFF THE ROOF

Speaking of oral sex and changing one's mind, many men experience the latter when the occasion for the former falls during the time when **a woman has her period. If such a man, at such a time, declines to perform such an act, is it such a crime?**

No. In fact, most women choose to abstain from intercourse entirely during that time anyway. While that may strike some men as a case of throwing the baby out with the bath water, it does indicate the extent to which women consider their periods a time for the suspension of the usual sexual rules.

Of course, there are men who find the whole thing a turn-on. If the woman enjoys it, in spite of (or because of) thinking her man a bit weird, so much the better.

WHAT DO YOU MEAN, "THAT WAS GREAT"?

It's no secret that men and women have, generally speaking, different capacities—should we say "timetables"? —for attaining climax during sex. Nature, whatever Her nefarious reasons, has seen to it that men get there more readily than women. This may have served well the purpose of propagating the species as a whole, but it often leaves certain women feeling frustrated and disappointed, and certain men feeling guilty and inadequate.

Frustration, guilt, disappointment, inadequacy: this is a job for Etiquette. Not that *Mayflower Manners* can provide useful tips on technique—it will have you know it's not that kind of book—but it can ask, **Is it rude for a man to fail to satisfy a woman?**

Admittedly, the question itself has its flaws. It may be that sexual satisfaction is not something a man succeeds or fails in "providing" for a woman, but is something the two of them pursue together. It's also arguable that "rude" is too puny a term for so cataclysmic an encounter, and that the traditional remedy for rudeness—a gracious apology—is hardly adequate to the situation. Granting both objections, still: **Is it a breach of whatever we mean by sexual etiquette for a man to leave a woman unsatisfied?**

It is if, after having his fun, he goes about his postcoital business (sleeping, grabbing a snack from the kitchen, etc.) without regard for her feelings; and it is if, after intercourse, he refuses to try other methods—which he should do after a reasonable interval of rest. Say, a few minutes. If he "forgets" to, or if she is really aroused and "hanging," and she feels it necessary to make an urgent request, she should avoid sounding angry or self-righteous or demanding, all of which will provoke a resentful or sullen response and pollute the atmosphere. Instead, she should try being playful or flattering (she might mention his "magic fingers" or "special kisses"— make up your own silly terms if you don't like these). She is entitled to want something from him, but not to blame him.

In return for not being blamed, he should be—or, at least, act—enthusiastic. This, of course, can be difficult, if all his desire has disappeared with his climax. But let him imagine how she feels, and let him bear in mind that Nature's imperfect physiological wiring scheme of the two sexes notwithstanding, fair is fair.

IT'S ALL IN THE, UH, WRIST

Everybody has their repertoire of "moves," even if for some people they consist of lying dead still and waiting for the whole ordeal to be over. Thus the question arises: What if you don't like what your partner does? That is, **If you don't like the way your partner kisses, or caresses, or etc., is it acceptable to say so?** Or is any hint of criticism automatically insulting and bad bed manners?

Obviously, if your partner causes you (unwanted) pain, you're entitled to respond. Such comments and observations as "Ow!" and "Not so hard!" are perfectly within the bounds of courteous discourse. If, however, you happen to dislike your partner's specific techniques, your responses should take the form of requests for something else. "You know what?" you are "suddenly" inspired to say, "Why don't you try [etc.]?" Or, "I just love it when you [etc.]." (Be sure, if you can, you are speaking to someone who has in fact [etc.] with you before.) When at a loss, try pseudo-wistful longing, e.g., "I've always wondered what it would be like if you would [etc.]," bearing in mind that "always" means, in this case, "suddenly in the last few seconds."

PRO OR CON A QUID PRO QUO

And then there are the people for whom sex is a sort of exalted exchange of intimate favors, a supercharged version of "You scratch my back, I'll scratch yours." Does such swap-meet bartering have a place in Mayflower Mannerly sex? Put briefly, **If A does X to B, is B obliged to do X to A?**

No. If A does X in the expectation that he/she will therefore be entitled to have it done to him/her—to, as it were, *force* B to do it in return—then the essential freedom that underlies all good manners is violated. A is in that case practicing coercion ("I'm not going to do it to you unless you promise to do it to me") or extortion ("You have to do it to me. I just did it to you, didn't I?"). Neither has a place in polite society, sexual or otherwise.

OOH LA LA (LA, LA, ETC.)

Mindful that the subject can quickly expand beyond comprehension into an infinite number of combinations and permutations, let us still ask, **Are there basic principles of etiquette that apply to the ménage à trois and ménage à quatre?**

Yes, but let not the reader get excited. They're as applicable to a child's birthday party as to a bed full of adults. For threesomes, the basic principles are, Everyone should take part willingly, and No one should show favoritism. There should be no pouting accusations, afterward, of "You never do that to me, but you did to her."

As for foursies, the principle of voluntary participation holds even more strongly. It's also important that no one be jealous or possessive (this restates the first rule, actually, but can't be emphasized enough), and that "safe sex" practices be observed.

Sometimes the *quatres* break up into two *folies à deux*,

at which point awkward French yields to good old American **swapping**.

If the participants are married, then it's wise to follow a rule forbidding mention of anyone's spouse, i.e., yours, or your partner's. At least, not until the reflective postcoital phase. It's awkward enough when the name of a third party comes up when two unmarried people are in bed. It's as though the third party has stepped into the room. Let the phantom third party be someone's husband or wife, whom both partners know to be present in the next room (with the *other* partner's spouse), and the bed starts to fill up with ghosts. What's the point? Everyone might just as well call the whole sex thing off and gather around a table for bridge.

This, of course, doesn't pertain if the sexual activity is of the institutionalized, organized sort called "swinging," in which case the relevant etiquette for sex is the same as that for a party in the home.

GOING TO, AND COMING FROM, EXTREMES
Having broached the subject of group sex, *Mayflower Manners* might as well bite the bullet and ask, **Are there any general principles of etiquette applicable to extreme, or more sophisticated, activity?** Or do people indulge in extreme forms of sexuality precisely to escape the chafing, nagging restrictions of etiquette?

Granted that to some, "extreme behavior" may mean having sex with the lights on or one's eyes open, in this case it refers to that range of activities (and equipment) that lie beyond normal, everyday heterosexual intercourse: role playing of dominance and submission, bondage and discipline, sadomasochism, whips and chains, etc. Much of this activity takes place in a professional context—at "houses" and "parlors," or with visiting "mistresses" and "masters," in which case etiquette yields to the house rules.

When pursued by intimates, though, some principles of good manners can be said to apply.

Start by being nonjudgmental. If your partner has taken to hinting about an interest in nonmainstream forms of sexuality, you are under no obligation to agree with it or pretend it attracts you too. But adopting a judgmental attitude can only shut off lines of communications between the two of you. Your partner, possibly embarrassed and insecure himself, will become more so, and may withdraw. You will be offended and disillusioned. None of this equals a recipe for pleasure. Decline, if you so choose, yes. Condemn, no.

Conversely, the one doing the proposing is advised to tread gently and not to pressure the other. Nonmainstream sexuality is not something a nervous partner "will get used to"; even as he indulges you in it, the risk is great that he will begin storing up reserves of resentment. He has a right not to like it. Pushing it on him, by whatever means, will probably only result in his anger or alienation. Talk about it, by all means; but avoid placing blame, making demands, judging him negatively, or making him feel weird or inadequate.

DIG THAT CRAZY SCENE

Some readers, distressed at how many aspects of sex are subject to some form of etiquette or another, may find themselves longing for one that isn't. Surely in kinky sex, they might think, we can find the wild and woolly, laissez-faire, if-it-feels-good-do-it spirit that prevailed in the Garden of Eden, before religion, Freud, and feminism came along to spoil the fun. Right?

Not right. If by "kinky" the reader thinks he or she means sadism and masochism (S&M), or bondage and discipline (B&D), then what he/she probably really means is **dominance and submission (D&S)**. S&M in its pure form is practiced by relatively few people, most of whom have serious emotional problems and pursue it for pathological reasons. B&D, meanwhile, is what goes on within the larger context of D&S. It is the classic whips-and-chains form of radical sexual role playing—and is, paradoxically, as replete with rules and protocols as a State Department reception.

D&S is a form of role playing in which fantasies of power or powerlessness, grandeur or worthlessness, control or helplessness, are acted out in a generally sexual context. It would seem, on the surface, that the dominant partner (the "Master" or "Mistress," depending on gender) determines what the submissive one (the "Slave") will or will not do or submit to. This is erroneous. In fact it is the Slave who has the last word about how things will go, since it is he or she who knows how much he/she can (or will) tolerate.

Taking part in such a fantasy is called "doing a scene." It is not necessarily sexual, although it often is, nor does it necessarily culminate in a sexual act, although it often does. In any case, partners doing a scene must have a code word or phrase for "you must absolutely stop right now," which the Slave may verbalize and the Master must obey immediately. It should not be too conventional: Phrases like "No," "Please stop," or "No more" may be integral to the scene itself, and consequently not be taken literally. Should the slave be gagged or otherwise unable to speak (having, e.g., been ordered to remain silent), he or she should hold a set of keys in his/her hand, which can be dropped to signal "stop."

As for those **whips and chains**: The former are used more for their effect as props, looking mean and sounding harsh, than to inflict any serious pain or injury. For precisely this reason, a Master/Mistress owes it to the Slave to be skilled in their use. The latter are used to bind and constrain the Slave, during which activity the Master/Mistress is absolutely forbidden to do anything the Slave would not willingly (notwithstanding histrionic objections) submit to. It's not exactly the Golden Rule—Master/Mistress and Slave are in fact busily engaged in doing things unto each other they have no desire to have done unto them—but more like an Iron Rule: Do unto others as you know they would be done unto, and then cool it.

The popular image of such goings-on usually involves an unaccompanied male (usually a "respectable businessman") patronizing a "house," where a leather-clad dominatrix awaits to insult, degrade, and whip him, for a fee. In fact, though, many couples enjoy doing scenes—yes, and **doing them in public, i.e., with each other, at clubs or private parties**. Etiquette, as always, plays a central role. After all, this is not some squalid little thing you do by yourself in your room when nobody is looking. This is sex (of a sort), with a partner, out in society, and its principles of ritual politesse rival those of a Japanese geisha establishment.

Below, therefore, some basic observations.

DOMINANCE AND SUBMISSION: BASIC ETIQUETTE TIPS

(Copy and Save for Future On-the-Spot Reference)

AT THE CLUB: HOW TO MIX AND MINGLE

1. Never touch, or otherwise engage, another's Slave without his/her Master's/Mistress's express permission.

2. A Master/Mistress may invite the Master/Mistress of another Slave to join him/her (and his/her Slave) in a scene. If so asked, be sure to determine the exact parameters of your involvement in the scene. If necessary, ask the host Master/Mistress. Err on the side of the conservative.

3. You may request to join another couple in a scene, thus: Master/Mistress of Couple 1 (M1) says to Master/Mistress of Couple 2 (M2), "What a beautiful [corset/collar/whatever] your Slave is wearing." This presents M2 the opportunity to say, if he/she wants to, "Why, thank you. Would you like to [see it/touch it/etc.]?" Eye contact and (according to one source) "an interested facial expression" between Masters/Mistresses are also quite proper.

However, a Master/Mistress never initiates eye contact with another's Slave.

An alternate method involves one Slave approaching the other's Master. The Slave's Master then approaches his/her counterpart, and the two of them negotiate the parameters of the scene.

4. At a club, a couple may encounter unaccompanied Slaves, ninety-five percent of whom are men. Proper etiquette requires an unaccompanied Slave to seek to

join a couple by approaching the Master/Mistress. Unaccompanied Slaves must be nonthreatening and respectful. (And, let's face it: if they're not, who is?) The most common way an unaccompanied Slave seeks entrée to a couple is to request to worship the feet—not "at the feet," no, the literal pedal appendages—of the coupled Slave. It's considered (for some reason) nonsexual, nonthreatening, and respectful.

5. A Master/Mistress is not obligated to include his/her Slave in a scene with another Master-Slave couple, nor is it rude if he/she declines to offer them the use of his/her Slave in return afterward.

6. Staring, watching, etc., are permissible. Indeed, they are integral to the scene being conducted at a party or club. But all viewing must be respectful. Expressions of amusement, disgust, disapprobation, revulsion, hilarity, horror, etc., are extremely impolite. Observers must be nonjudgmental.

7. First names only are used. They need not necessarily be participants' real names. It is impolite to ask a person's real name, or last name.

8. Never give out the real name or phone number of another person. Discretion is paramount.

IN THE HOME: HOW TO HOST OR ATTEND A PARTY

1. Ninety-nine percent of all guests are couples. However, some Masters/Mistresses will have multiple Slaves who may or may not be of the same sex.

2. Do not be "fashionably late." The evening commences with the guests mingling and socializing, becom-

ing (re)acquainted and getting comfortable with each other. Latecomers impede this process.

3. Six to eight couples is an optimal number of guests. Couples can feature all Masters, all Mistresses, or mixed. The host Master/Mistress will have his/her Slave(s) do almost all the work, although it is not uncommon to "borrow" the Slaves of others to help out. Guest Slaves are not *expected* to pitch in, however, and should not do so unless (their Master/Mistress is) asked, as otherwise their unsolicited assistance might impugn the competence of the host Slave.

4. Such affairs usually feature a buffet dinner. An offer to bring food, or wine or champagne, coordinated with the host, is most appreciated.

5. The host Slave is *not* like a waiter or a waitress. If you want something brought to you, you'll just have to endure the inconvenience of asking your own Slave to get it. And if you are a Slave, why then you must get it for yourself, of course—after first asking permission from your own Master/Mistress.

6. If the host Slave brings something to a guest, it is gracious to say "thank you" but not considered rude if you don't.

7. The host Slave should serve all the Masters and Mistresses first, and then their Slaves, unless the host Master/Mistress has made it clear that the guest Slaves may help themselves.

8. It is not necessary to "do" anything, such as take part in a scene. Some couples are content to merely observe; some will interact only with each other. Still, most will interact to at least a small extent with others.

9. After the preliminary socializing, the Masters/Mistresses will usually have their Slaves disrobe down to their "outfits," or change into "something more comfortable." The Masters/Mistresses will usually have some sort of specialized apparel on, too.

10. As with any party, a thank-you note or a phone call afterwards is appropriate and appreciated.

LADIES, OR GENTLEMEN, FIRST

So much for the kinky stuff. Getting back to ordinary, everyday, down-home, garden-variety sexual intercourse, one finds oneself wondering, for the first if not the ten tousandth time, **Is it more polite for the man to wait until the lady reaches orgasm, before doing so himself? Or doesn't order matter?**

Yes, the question is a bit disingenuous. Some men are able to "wait" as long as it takes, some strive mightily and succeed in waiting X minutes but find X + 1 beyond them, and some are able to hold off only for much shorter intervals. The reality of the matter is that how long either party is able to hold off or hasten orgasm is largely out of his or her control. What is being addressed here, then, is the principle of the thing.

But then, this is a case in which principle follows reality. In terms of etiquette, order doesn't matter. It may be appealing, for whatever reason, to have the man wait for the woman to climax first—or, as was considered optimal in the 1950s, for both to orgasm at the same time. But, faced with the vagaries of men's and women's physiology, psychology, and neurology, and wised up by three decades of sexological research, *Mayflower Manners* elects to lighten up and let everyone off the hook. (For having sex while on the hook, see "Extremes," above.)

Good manners consist of looking after the behavior you yourself can control. If a man wants to let his partner climax first, and is able to, more power to him (and her). If not, he is only obliged to try alternate means after his own climax (see "Will You, Won't You," above). If a woman can reach orgasm first, fine. If not—and, according to one source, less than 50 percent of all women are able to attain climax during normal intercourse, whatever "normal" means—her only obligation is to tell her partner, after a reasonable amount of time spent trying other ways, if no amount of activity on his part will avail.

In etiquette, one does what one should, but one does what one can. It is not bad manners to do something, or not do something, when you have no control over it.

SOMETIMES IT'S HARD TO GET UP IN THE MORNING

One of the many interesting differences between men and women concerns their readiness to have **sex in the morning,** i.e., many men possess this readiness, and many women do not. **How to resolve this conflict, when he wants to do it before they start their day, and she does not?**

In the short run, the tie goes to the one who is reluctant; her desire not to takes precedence over his desire to.

In the long run—i.e., in a relationship of any duration, in which sex is a part of a larger interaction—he has a right to expect his desires or needs to be acknowledged and satisfied. In that case, they should seek a compromise. One source suggests they refrain from sex on weekdays, but pursue it on weekends. Or every other day. Oh, let *them* figure it out.

GOOD CLEAN FUN

Some things are easier to talk about than others. Sex, formerly the great unmentionable in polite society, is these days (along with money and real estate) the great mentionable. But put two people in close proximity, take their clothes off, and observe how so basic and simple a topic as physical hygiene can bring on embarrassment. Thus the question, **What's a nice way for either partner to complain about the other's hygiene, or lack thereof?**

It is here that the basic jiujitsu of etiquette proves so useful. Rather than command the beloved to run into the shower, you implicitly "criticize" yourself: "Would you like to use the shower first, or should I?" The tone, of course, is one of routine presumption—your partner has, you imply, been expecting just this query all along.

If that seems too pedestrian and unromantic, merely spice up the essentially identical offer: "Taking a bath with you is my [favorite part of the day/favorite thing in the world/heart's desire/secret fantasy]." So saying, produce bubble bath, candles, vintage champagne, strolling violinists, etc. Women of course are more sanctioned in the business of frilling up the tub, which is why a man's doing it will make an even greater impact.

To make lasting changes in the routine of a partner and encourage more fastidious hygiene, follow-up is all-important. Be sure, with every bath or shower, to positively reinforce how sexy and appealing you find him/her when he or she is "squeaky clean." Praise his or her brand of soap, shampoo, etc., and be showily appreciative of how it adds to the attraction of those intimate places (i.e., of the body. Not charming little restaurants). You are dealing here not with conscious neglect, but habit. Be subtle but persistent.

IN THE HEAT OF THE NIGHTIE

Speaking of naked, sometimes it's like a Cunard steamship trip to Europe—getting there is half the fun. It becomes a bit more than half when the journey involves a stopover at **sexy negligees.** But the problem with such garments, with their see-throughs and peekaboos and half-hidden this and artfully revealed that, is that they threaten to work too well. The more provoking they are, the more they seem to beckon for their own destruction. Would such a fate—the ripping asunder of alluring lingerie at the hands of a frenzied, hyperaroused male—constitute a triumphant culmination, or a needlessly violent tragedy?

You can see how easy it is to get carried away talking about nighties. Put it this way: **Is it rude for a man to rip an erotic garment off a woman, or is it exactly what the woman seeks to provoke?**

It depends on how much the thing costs. Some of these little nothings go for a bundle, and their owner will not take kindly to their wanton destruction. Also, it depends on how actually "uncontrollable" they make the man. While *Mayflower Manners* has no interest in legislating how wild men and women are "allowed" to become during sex, men should nonetheless be aware that most women are at least a little uncomfortable in such garments. Leaping on her and tearing it off in a frenzy would probably alarm her, and make her feel very uncomfortable and "dirty." Men should therefore not only try to resist destroying their partner's froufrou, but they should also take care to provide positive reinforcement about how she looks in it.

Especially if he wants her to wear it again.

But, someone will suggest, if I tear it into shreds in a fit of amorous arousal, all I have to do is buy her another one. After all, **it's an appropriate gift for a man to give a woman, isn't it?**

Well, it rather depends on how well he knows her, doesn't it? Not only because it's an intimate gift, but because the better he knows her, the more likely he is to know whether she'll feel comfortable in one or not. In fact, before actually buying a garter belt, a G-string, an underwire lacy bra, etc., the man would be well advised to sound out how much his partner would like one. Many women would be horrified and embarrassed at such gifts, accusing their partner of wanting them to "look like a whore." Others might be insecure about one part of their bodies or another (their thighs, say), and feel less than thrilled about a skimpy little teddy that shows them to (dis)advantage.

One way to avoid such misunderstandings is to look through some relevant catalogs (Victoria's Secret, Frederick's of Hollywood, etc.), discover what each partner finds appealing, and, in the words of one source, "compromise, compromise, compromise."

"Oh, hell," that same someone will complain. "Who

wants to compromise when it comes to naughty underwear? This is *sex* we're talking about!"

No it's not. It's women's clothing. ("Sex" is what happens when the clothing is removed.) For men to act presumptuously when it comes to such a subject is to court disaster.

FAST TIMES
In this era of fast computers, fast money, and fast food, one sometimes finds oneself wondering: **Is there really such a thing as a quickie? Is it okay, or insulting, to propose one?** (Is it just the short version of a normal proposition, or is it too brusquely unromantic, like asking, "Will you be my first wife?")

The good news is, there is such a thing. The bad news—not all that bad, really—is that you've got to get the timing right. There are moments when even a quickie is inappropriate: when she's just spent over an hour on her hair and makeup, when he's rushing to work or a tee-off reservation, or, of course, vice versa: he's taken forever to make up, she's en route to business or sports.

Or when one partner is not in the mood. Quickies may be quick, but they're intense.

SEX MEANS NEVER HAVING TO SAY YOU'RE SORRY YOU'RE NOT IN LOVE
Around the age of thirteen or so, the canny youth (let's say she is a girl, although it holds for boys, too) begins to realize that much of the time, in song lyrics, in book titles, on magazine covers, and in movies and on TV, the word "love" does not mean love. It means sex. (Ac-

tually, these days, this realization probably arrives at about the age of eight.) The puzzled young adolescent to whom "A Night of Love" seemed to mean (improbably) a night of necking, hand-holding, and taking moony walks, discovers in an illuminating flash one day that it really means a night of sex, a night in bed, a night of Doing It.

This revelation will dispel a great deal of mental fog that had accumulated ever since the child figured out what sex was. It will seem, in fact, that now she knows everything. But another surprise is in store. Whenever she starts having sex—*Mayflower Manners* is afraid to ask what the minimum age for kids is these days—she will feel a great desire to express the excitement, passion, and, yes, affection she feels during the act. She might want to say, "I love you!" Afterwards, she may reflect that she didn't really mean "love" in the romantic, moony-walk sense. But there seemed to be no viable alternative. She certainly couldn't have said, "I sex you!" could she?

This problem will persist for the rest of her life, and will arise whenever she is having sex with someone with whom she is not in love. She will wonder, as everyone else wonders, **Can you say "I love you" during sex, even if you don't mean it literally? And if someone says it to you, what do you say? Must you say it back?**

Let no one accuse *Mayflower Manners* of linguistic persnicketiness when it replies: You may say anything but "I love you," unless you really love the person. "I adore you," for example, is permissible, but is admittedly too contrived to gasp in the heat of passion. And if all the ardent, if semicoherent, lover's expressions ("Oh, yes!"

etc.) seem not direct or meaningful enough, still: Reserve the declaration of love for when it is meant literally—for when, that is, you want to say it out of bed. One can never know when one's sexual partner will take one literally, and conceive a definition of the relationship radically different than one's own.

And if you are the partner to whom "I love you" is uttered during sex, resist the temptation to say it back. It is not "polite" to return the sentiment if you don't truly feel it. Granted, "thank you" is a bit formal and stiff. You may fudge the issue, though, with various heartfelt but unspecific compliments: "You're gorgeous," "You're wonderful," and so on.

PLAYING AROUND BETWEEN CLASSES

America is a classless society in the sense that the tooth fairy is a historical personage. And you don't have to be British to know that often a great sexual attraction exists between **members of different classes**: a stockbroker dating a waitress, a financial analyst dating a garage mechanic, a business executive squiring an actress or an artist—everyone may comment about it, but no one wonders why they do it. **Is there an etiquette to such behavior?** And if you are a friend of either party, and **believe that one or the other is "using" his or her partner, may you intervene and say so?**

First things first: What is proper between two people of differing classes is more an ethical than an etiquette question, and concerns not their contrasting socioeconomic status so much as their relative degrees of sophistication and awareness. Let us merely suggest that it is wrong to conduct a relationship with someone under false pretenses, to lead them on, to pretend to a quality of interest that you do not truly feel.

As for the latter question, it is not as contrived as it sounds. Everyone is familiar with the scenario of the upper-class man or woman exploiting his or her lower-class paramour: pretending to an interest, or respect, or love, that is not real, solely to gain sexual favors. If you are a friend of either party and perceive such a drama being enacted, you might feel that somehow things aren't fair—that either intellectually or experientially, one person is no match for the other.

Conversely, you might believe that the upper-class partner is in sexual thrall to his/her lover, who is in turn only interested in the other's wealth. In either case, you might feel tempted to speak up.

Don't. Unless one party is truly and demonstrably a manipulating, heartless liar, stay out of it. What takes place between two people in a sexual relationship occurs on a plane inaccessible to onlookers. Your "objective" criticism, or well-intentioned warnings, or "innocent" observations, can only elicit one of two responses: Your friend will either turn defensive and resent you, or, if you are proven correct, feel humiliated in the presence of your superior knowledge. Who needs it?

ON THE OUTS WITH THE OLD IN-OUT
And then there's **celibacy**. It's not getting as much press as it used to, but that may be because a specific form of doing nothing is always less interesting to the media than some form—any form—of doing something. Still, **is someone's celibacy a fit topic for discussion?**

Only if he brings it up. Will the reader think *Mayflower Manners* cynical if it wonders if many instances of "celibacy" are more passive than active, more accepted than embraced—that is, more a state of being too depressed, fearful, or disheartened to look for sex, than one of voluntarily forswearing it? In any case, discuss another's celibacy only at his instigation—and do so nonjudgmentally, without scoffing, puzzlement, or applause. (Especially the latter—how will he look you in the eye when he falls, or jumps, off the wagon?)

BUT SOFT!

Presumably there are readers who thus far have felt they can live without the above discussion of sexual etiquette: "I have a normal sex life, and don't need any of those contrived, weird what-ifs." Fine. But they'll come crawling back on the day they, or their partners, prove **impotent or frigid**. If ever there were a situation in which all present wanted desperately to know the right thing to do and say, it is when the man cannot attain an erection or the woman cannot respond sexually. **How does one, as it were, "handle" it?**

Neither should blame the other, and neither should blame himself or herself. The concept of "fault" should be left outside the bedroom. Instead, he might say something like "You look so beautiful and sexy I guess I just can't believe my good luck. Can I have a raincheck?" (Let the woman to whom such comments seem feeble and insufficient ask herself whether she'd rather he say, "Well, my God, you're so demanding and voracious, of *course* I can't get it up!") She might then respond with "You promise?" and resist the temptation to ask him to perform alternative services. If he volunteers, she should not turn him down unless she really isn't inclined to continue. It is important, especially if this has happened before, for the woman to reassure the man that she cares for him and finds him desirable; to suggest otherwise will only exacerbate the problem.

In contrast, most women will enjoy the sexual act even if they're not truly aroused: the closeness, caring, and mutual affection will be enough. (At least for a while.) But he should ask if she wants to continue, and not assume. If her lack of responsiveness persists, they should discuss it outside the bedroom.

SHE'LL BE LYIN' THROUGH HER TEETH, NOW, WHEN SHE "COMES"

That women may still enjoy the general atmospherics of sex without actually being aroused by intercourse may strike some—viz., men—as being "unfair." On the other hand, women may reasonably complain that men reach climax far more easily than they. Men might counter with the observation that women are capable of multiple orgasms, which for men remains a sort of mythic, millennial ideal. Women might reply that at least men don't have to worry about getting pregnant.

This sort of oh-yeah/sez-who exchange of accusations may and perhaps should go on for the rest of human history. If it does, at some point someone will mention the fact that **women can fake orgasm much more easily than men. Is that a good thing, a bad thing, or simply a parlor trick?** Put another way, **Is it bad manners to fake it?**

Why, yes, it is. Bad manners, that is. It's a form of sexual lying, and like most lying creates far more problems than it solves. To be blunt, faking orgasm conveys the message that the man is satisfying the woman. If, after a while, she wants him to try different things to truly satisfy her, he'll be understandably confused—not to mention, when he puts two and two together, angry, embarrassed, and so forth. And even if she is content to go on simulating orgasm, how can it not create a distance between the two of them? How can her opinion of him be unaffected by his obliviousness of the truth? Clearly, faking orgasm for women is impolite, as well as impolitic.

As for men, faking orgasm is improbable: How, after all that strenuous activity and those sound effects, does one explain the persistence, in an unchanged state, of Exhibit A?

THAT'S ENTERTAINMENT?

You go to his place after or for some suitable refreshment, one thing leads or has already led to another, and in the course of things he produces a videocassette and slips it suavely into the player. You glance at the screen expecting to see a romantic or comic classic, but as you settle in to relax and enjoy a cozily amorous mood, what you see instead is *Indiana's Jones and the Lust Crusade*, or *The Man Who Came at Dinner*, or *The Hard-On Is a Lonely Hunter*—in a word, **X-rated (i.e., "dirty") movies**. About which you are not exactly crazy. **What do you do?**

You do not make your host feel depraved or weird. Rather than issue judgmental opinions which might insult him, you accept the "blame" yourself. Tell him it makes you uncomfortable, hinting that the shortcoming is not in his good taste (although you may think it is), but in your delicate constitution.

He, in return, should comply readily, and not make a big deal ("But I paid two-fifty to rent this!") about turning it off.

NO STOCK IN BONDAGE

But now suppose that rather than a pornographic movie on the tube, you notice **bondage equipment in the bedroom**. Unless your reaction is along the lines of "Oh, boy!" or even "Well, maybe . . ." you might want to state for the record that **you're not interested. Do you do so now, or when your host suggests that somebody start buckling up? And, for God's sake, how?**

As in the case of the blue movie above, it is important not to insult your host. Rather than point and cry, "Me? In *that*? You're sick!" allow as how your own idiosyncratic proclivities prevent you from approaching such activity with any real degree of relish. Or, simply say, "It's not for me." And it would be better to do so before things get under way, when both heads are cool and capable of reason. Besides, if you are indisposed to use the gear, its presence will distract you until you mention it. But you might try asking what its use entails; it might not be as bad as you think, and even if it is—or worse—you can thereupon say no, thank you.

If you are the host whose fantasy of tying, or being tied, up has been shattered, strive to take it graciously. Stifle your disappointment and withhold all scornful remarks about your partner's lack of adventurousness. Yes, all this is self-evident—but often when sexual experimentation . . . well, *crops up*, people tend to get self-righteous. The person proposing the activity feels a sort of macho (or macha) pride in going beyond the boundaries of normal sexual conduct; the one declining the activity feels that he or she is being asked to violate themselves in a particularly intimate, and therefore egregious, manner. Thus, this reminder to mind your p's and q's when someone mentions B&D.

ASSAULT WITH, OR ON, A DEAD WEAPON

One of the most disconcerting experiences in daily life, aside from anticipating a terrific sneeze and having someone come along and startle you out of it, is the sudden realization, while working ardently to arouse your sex partner, that **it's not working**. The telltale sounds, the languorous movements, the urgent gestures: they're conspicuous in their absence. **How long ought one to continue in the face (or whatever it is) of such absence of results? And what should the one not responding say?**

The party who is receiving the attention has a duty to tell his/her partner (as soon as it becomes clear) either (a) what should be done differently, if something else will work, or (b) to relax and take five, if nothing is going to work. A light touch, and a sensitivity to the arouser's feelings, are paramount at such times. Meaning: Be sure to get across the point that it has nothing to do with your partner (even—perhaps especially—if it does), but that you just aren't in the mood. If your partner is obviously raring to go, you might offer to please him or her in another way, but only if you really want to.

If you are the one whose attentions are being declined,

try to take it like a man, or like a woman. Your partner's reasons may be valid, no matter how frustrated you feel. And don't press for an alternate solution unless you're prepared to risk his/her resentment. Of course, if this scene is enacted many times, it should be discussed outside the bedroom, perhaps with a counselor.

A DELICATE ISSUE

Abortion is perhaps the most controversial sex-related topic in America today. Short of taking an official position either in favor of a woman's right to choose to have one or against, *Mayflower Manners* would be remiss if it did not ask, on behalf of those women (and, secondarily, their partners) for whom it is an option: **Should the man offer to accompany the woman? And should he offer to pay for it?**

Obviously, whether or not a woman should have an abortion is not a topic to which etiquette is relevant. The man's deportment and financial involvement, however, are. Let us say that when a woman elects to have such a procedure, the man should make himself as available as possible. He should offer to accompany her. He should offer to pay all, not half, the cost. Regardless of what her partner does, she will "pay" for the procedure in numerous ways, many of which might persist for the rest of her life. Holding her hand, and paying the bill, are literally the least the man can do. If, of course, she prefers to be accompanied by a girlfriend, to pay half, etc., those are her rights. But he should at least ask.

G-MAN ON PATROL!

Remember the **"G-spot"**? *Mayflower Manners* does, if vaguely. For those for whom it remains the bull's-eye of

female sexual stimulation, then, this poignant query:
**Should the well-meaning lover doggedly poke around
for it?**

No.

AND WOULD EITHER OF YOU CARE FOR MORE RUMAKI?

Finally, this business of **people having sex at parties:
What does the well-meaning host(ess) do upon dis-
covering two guests in flagrante delicto in the bedroom, media room, rumpus room, etc.?** On the one
hand, they're guests. On the other hand, they're indulging (with both hands) in a pleasure which, probably
by definition, they will be unable to share with the other
guests. Do you scream bloody murder and banish them
from the premises? Invoke homeowner's privilege and
join in? Summon the others for a rousing, "fun" group
activity? Offer to refresh their drinks?

None of the above, alas. You discreetly shut the door
and let them finish. The next day, or the next hour, take
aside the one to whom you're closest, and ask him or
her not to do it again. Or, if you think the whole thing
is something of a hoot, you may proceed to tease the
person about it for the next few weeks, if not decades.

$\mathscr{A}$FFAIRS

In General: $\mathscr{B}$y "affairs," *Mayflower Manners* means not "love affairs," or foreign affairs, but extramarital affairs. That "extra" doesn't mean "super-duper," as in "Extra-Strength Tylenol"; no, it means "outside of." The subject is illegal affairs. One knows this. And one knows that in traversing such terrain, at every step of the way Etiquette proceeds under the dour scowl of disapproval of its older brother, Ethics. "Go ahead," Ethics mutters. "Talk about politeness in the commission of a crime. But don't ask me to get involved or give you my blessing."

This is the voice of conscience, and rare is the lover enmeshed in an affair who has not yearned to answer it with a heartfelt, "Oh, shut up." It won't, usually, but there are those who wish to do the right, mannerly thing even while suffering its disapproval. For them, this.

[Note: In what follows, the assumption is that one partner in the affair is married—the man, probably— and the other is single. When both partners are married, the rules below continue to apply, but in stereo.]

I GOT (IN THE CONTEXT OF BEING MARRIED TO HER) YOU, BABE

One issue which proved a veritable hornets' nest when it was broached to sources was **who rightfully should propose an affair to whom.** The overwhelming consensus was that the married person should propose it to the single person. Many women expressed sharp disapproval of other women who charge forward and pursue men regardless of whether the man is married or even seeing someone regularly. This was universally held to be bad form.

Inseparable from this stricture is one which holds that the married person must announce, from the beginning, his or her status. This especially if he is a man, and wears no wedding ring. He or she may also mention if the married couple is close to a divorce.

GOING THROUGH A BLATANCY PERIOD

One of the more thrilling scenarios in the lives of the very wealthy is the spectacle of one spouse appearing in public—in society—with his or her paramour while the other spouse, or friends, stare aghast. Maybe the wealthy can get away with such shenanigans, but can regular people like the reader? Not hardly. That's why it's bad affair manners to **display an affair in the presence of the spouse, or the spouse's (or the couple's) friends**. This is anywhere from unsporting to downright cruel to the spouse; meanwhile, the couple's friends are placed in a frightful bind when confronted with this blatant infidelity. And their discomfort must communicate itself to the unmarried lover. What a terrible idea! Don't do it.

A SMALL CIRCLE OF FRIENDS

Now you are the single person involved with the married one, and in the course of some discreet socializing you are introduced to **his unmarried friends, or to couples with whom he shares confidences. Can you establish a relationship with them**, or are you de facto a priori persona non grata?

Please excuse *Mayflower Manners'* showing off its Latin. As to the answer, yes, you may develop a relationship with them—that is, you have every right to want to. If they are inclined to reciprocate, all well and good. If they are not—if their behavior toward you is disapproving, for example—try to find some consolation in the fact that they are being rude. The ethical subtext of things notwithstanding—and you have a case to make that their disapproval should be directed toward your lover more than you—good manners require them to behave well regardless.

If you do establish a relationship with them, however, bear in mind that their first allegiance may be to your lover's wife—this, no matter how close you and they become. If you want to retain their affection, demonstrate on those occasions when they must choose between you and her, and they choose her, that you know they are doing what they must. Insisting that they abandon her for you will probably lead to an opposite outcome.

WHAT A "COINCIDENCE"!

One paradox of extramarital affairs is the possessiveness felt by the unmarried member of the trio. This sometimes inspires her (or him) to monitor the movements of the lover and spouse, and even results in her **showing up at parties, dinners, etc. which she knows the couple will also be attending. Is that okay?**

That is the opposite of okay. It may be understandable, from the point of view of a jealous or insecure lover, but as a display of manners it is inappropriate. As in the case of the husband's flaunting the affair in public, everyone suffers: Your lover is caught in an emotional vise, his wife is (if she is unaware of the affair) sure to sense something amiss (and if she does know of it, is sure to be furious at your provocation), and friends who know the score will be appalled. Entertained, yes, and provided with a month's worth of gossip thereafter, certainly, but appalled.

Is that what you want? If it is, you got it. But mannerswise, you ain't got it.

ESPOUSING PROPER BEHAVIOR

And how should the person in an affair behave toward his (or her) own spouse? The claim that etiquette applies in such a situation may ring a little hollow, but still: There are things one does, and does not, do. One does not rub the spouse's nose in the details of the affair if she knows about it. One does not deliberately provoke her suspicions, either by displaying evidence directly to her or by being observed by her friends (unless one is at the mercy of his own unconscious desire to be found out).

And one is absolutely scrupulous about protecting the spouse's health with regard to sexually transmitted diseases.

FOR ME? OH, YOU *SHOULD* HAVE

Finally, this less than romantic note: Many sources said that when in an affair with a married man, they expected —and received—"compensation" for those occasions when the man went off with his wife on trips, vacations, etc. Such emoluments included jewelry, fur coats, or expenses-paid trips for the woman and a friend. If the men didn't offer, they hinted until he came through.

Apparently, then, it is good manners to give your lover a little, or a big, something as a consolation prize when you are to be otherwise engaged. One source commented, "Not that many people have their rent paid any more," but considering what rent is in New York, Los Angeles, etc., it's small wonder.

IN
BETWEEN

PETS

In General: **M**uch as we love them, or much as people we know love them, and despite an ironic saying to the contrary, cats and dogs are *not* people, too. It conveys no disrespect to our feline and canine "friends" to state that people are people, and cats and dogs are animals. It's worth noting this normally self-evident truth because there are individuals out there, whom one occasionally meets, visits, dates, etc., who love their pets as much as—oh, let's say it: more than—any human being in their lives. That is their prerogative, of course; the difficulty comes when they treat a guest with less deference than they do their toy schnauzer, or, what is worse, expect the guest to dote on Schatzi as much as they.

What makes this dilemma especially irritating is the galling little catch-22 hidden within it. Quite often, those people who adore their pets at the expense of their guests are people who live alone—i.e., the very ones most eligible for, and possibly most in need of, cultivating a long-term relationship. It stands to reason, of course: being by themselves, they confide in the pet, take solace from its benign presence, tease it, nurture it, complain to it, etc. The pet is their ally, child, superego, pal, partner in crime, conscience, and so on—but it's all one-dimensional. A person talking to a cat is a person talking to himself. With the possible exception of some very clever parrots, no pet will demonstrate either the will or the ability to prod one's thinking, challenge one's assumptions, or even add to one's store of topical jokes.

Then a visitor comes along, and the pet owner, accustomed to one-way conversations and blanket (if nonverbal) support, is called upon to engage in dialogue. Often the primary topic about which the pet owner is prepared to wax enthusiastic and fascinated is . . . the pet. And it's downhill from there. The visitor—who, let's say for the sake of illustration, does not own a pet himslf or herself—smiles politely and murmurs vacant phrases of interest over what, to him or her, seems like nothing more than an ordinary skulking gray-striped cat, or a typically annoying yapping Pekingese. The owner soon grows suspicious of the guest's inability to appreciate the manifold depths of this unique animal's appearance, personality, and soul. The guest feels emotionally extorted —as the saying has it, Love me, love my dog—the owner feels self-righteous, and only the animal itself escapes a sense of being wronged.

Who needs it? Guests of those with pets, who have in the past complained of such behavior with comments like "He treats his damn dog like it's his child, for God's sake," would do well to remember that the quickest way to win a parent's affection is to display some appreciation of his or her child. Pet owners, on the other hand, should remind themselves at least twice a day that their relationship with their animal, no matter how intense or how merited by the creature's objective virtues, is in fact entirely subjective. Your dazzlingly intelligent dog named Cat, your hilariously fussy cat named Mouse: To the world, they're just a couple of animals. Expecting visitors to swoon over them as you do can only lead to alienation: theirs from the animal, yours from them.

GOING TO BED WITH ANIMALS

The idea of a **dog or cat sleeping on a bed** during the night evokes a series of wholesome images: the trusty Irish setter sprawled across the feet of the innocent slumbering child, the dainty Siamese curled up near the night-gown-clad form of her mistress, etc. Fine. But if there is no child, and the mistress is accompanied by a friend, may the cat still curl up?

Only if the friend has been asked and, having been allowed to answer honestly, said yes. Otherwise, put out the cat. This is less a problem for owners whose friends are allergic to pets; such people have spent their lives not stroking cats, not frisking with dogs, and recoiling discreetly when the house animal rubs against their legs. They'll have no trouble asking that your pet sleep elsewhere.

But those not so afflicted might think it incumbent on them to answer, "Oh, sure," when their host says, "Coco always sleeps with me, and she'll be up all night destroying the living room if I kick her out. Is it okay if she stays?" Such a request is legitimate. But so is an answer in the negative, e.g., "Gee, I'd rather she didn't, actually." People, outrageous and even sometimes indefensible as it may seem, have precedence over pets. This is especially true of guests, who are advised, if asked the above question in a tone that seems not to allow for a negative reply, to answer, "Of course Coco can stay. But I'd really rather not sleep with an animal. Is it all right if I stay up all night and destroy the living room?"

But what if the host or hostess simply doesn't ask? What if, when sleep-time comes, he or she summons Prince or Chairman Meow and beds down as usual? May one protest?

Certainly. Etiquette may require politeness in the face of insult, but it doesn't mean having to let people (or their animals) walk (or sleep) all over you. However, a certain minimal politesse is called for. Rather than snarl, "My god, get that filthy beast out of here," say, in tones of regret, "I'm sorry, I'd really rather Prince didn't sleep in the bed." If the wording of that remark seems to suggest that the decision is yours to make, you're right. It is. Or should be.

NOTE TO PET-OWNING HOSTS: And it goes without saying—or with only saying once—that people who regularly sleep with a dog or a cat should change their linen before a night on which they expect to be sleeping with a human.

MY KENNEL, OR YOURS?
Rex Boxer and Catherine Katt have had dinner, have exchanged the appropriate signals both explicit and implicit, and have agreed to spend the night together. They hail a cab and climb in. And then they look at each other and, in the passion of the moment, each is compelled to reveal a hitherto secret piece of intimate information of which the other must be made aware immediately, lest their entire relationship be imperiled.

Rex, it turns out, has a beagle he has to walk "pretty soon." Catherine, who prefers sleeping at her own apartment, keeps a Persian for which she has left food and water.

Q: Where do they tell the driver to go?

A: To chez Boxer, at least as their first stop. The needs of a pet, and therefore of the pet's owner, play a legitimate role in the calculation of who joins whom to sleep where. Catherine's desire to speed to her place is outweighed by Rex's need to take "Bob" around the block.

People **dating people with pets**, therefore, find themselves having to adjust to a hierarchy of animal need. At least for a single night, dogs usually require more attention than cats, cats usually require more attention than fish, fish usually require more attention than nothing.

But what if both parties have pets needing equal attention?

Either of two solutions is possible. Either one animal must travel—preferably to the home of the person most able or willing to put up with the presence of an extra pet—or a preliminary stop must be made for the care of one pet before proceeding on to the home of the other.

Of course, this only holds for periods of a single evening. If the two wish to spend, say, a weekend together, they can either bring the animals together in a single place or spend time and effort and money volleying back and forth, several times a day, between each other's homes. Or, most convenient of all (and most expensive), they can agree to place one or both of the animals in a kennel, or farm them out to friends, in exchange for a promise to perform a similar favor some other day.

Of course, women and men seeking to avoid the inconveniences and awkwardnesses discussed above, while trying to build a relationship with someone, can avoid them entirely in a very simple way: by not having a pet. Indeed, there are those who insist that convenience aside, a pet distracts one's attention from the object of one's amorous, sexual, or matrimonial desire. "It's tough enough to find an eligible man," one lady has written, noting that "men require a great deal more attention than is commonly acknowledged." Still, she adds, it's worth the trade-off, since men "don't usually have accidents on your new carpet."

ENTERTAINING

In General: **W**hy on earth do people host parties, or invite others to their homes for dinner? On the surface there seems to be no compelling reason, other than the crude one of repaying previous invitations. And that, as a motive, is not very satisfying; balancing your social books, clearing your conscience, and laying the groundwork for being invited to future parties is all so abstract compared to the real, physical, arduous work required to prepare food, clean the house, and throw it open to the world. After all, unless you are content (and can afford) to have outside helpers and sources clean the house and bring in the food, you have to:

- Decide on the guest list. Match couples with singles, the simpatico with the irksome, the fun with the dull, the people you look forward to seeing with those whom you owe.
- Plan the menu, shop for ingredients, lug them home, and store them until you need them.
- Gear up your kitchen for preparing three, four, five, or more times what it normally does. This includes using not just your usual trusty old three pots and two pans, but every piece of equipment you can lay your increasingly desperate hands on, including the tarnished pressure cooker with the missing top and the loose handle, the rusted wok that won't come clean, the toy bread knife given as a gift by a relative who eats only Wonder

Bread, and the stupid punch bowl your mother foisted on you ten years ago.

• Clean the entire house or apartment, then decorate and primp and worry about the optimal arrangement of flowers, the strategic placement of magazines, etc.

• Cook with a vengeance and, worse, with a time-table. Endure a crisis of conscience about preparing something a week in advance and freezing it. Fret over whether to make enough, too much, or too too much.

• Keep cooking.

• Be showered and dressed in time to admit the first guest, while still cooking all the while. Hope the others are on time, or at least not so late as to imperil certain dishes.

• Pump up the guests to a self-sustaining level of joie de vivre.

• Serve drinks, and then food, and hope the gods of home entertainment are kind.

• Clear dinner plates and serve desserts while juggling coffee, tea, and cordial orders *and* stowing dirty dishes in the kitchen (or somewhere).

• Regulate the winding-down of everything, the good-byes, the awkward moments when some have left but others remain, and your sheer fatigue.

• Hope everyone's thanks are credible.

• Survey the carnage, and pray there are no secret casualties of which you are as yet unaware: an antique tabletop stabbed with a still-burning cigarette, a polished end table decorated with still-wet, uncoastered cocktail glasses, a missing TV remote control, a broken glass, etc.

• Wrap and store the salvageable leftovers.

• Clean up.

Put this way, hosting a party seems as attractive a prospect as root canal. Even with hired (or dragooned) help, you become a foreman, and must still oversee the entire list of tasks.

Still, just about everyone, sooner or later, does it. For those who enjoy cooking, the occasion presents an opportunity to flex the larger culinary muscles: You get to prepare things normally too grandiose or impractical—a fully loaded gumbo, a whole leg of lamb, etc. And even for those whose idea of home cooking is reheating takeout in the microwave, masterminding and executing a dinner can be enormously satisfying. You get to choose the guest list, for one thing, and you experience something of the thrill of control and power known to generals and film directors. You get to tell people what to do, what to eat, whom to sit next to—even, at times, what to talk about. And (incredibly) they do it. Not only that, but they thank you for the opportunity.

And if they have enjoyed themselves, you can feel a small measure of pride, because they have taken pleasure from a production of which you were principal author, director, and producer. If, in the course of staging the production, you get to show off a favorite recipe or some new decor, all the better. So, too, if you have accomplished some secret agenda: the introduction of two unmarried people, the advancement of a professional relationship, the dissemination of a devastating bit of gossip about a rival or enemy, the honoring of a friend, the celebration of a milestone.

You have also, perforce, cleaned your home (maybe for the first time in too long), placed others in your social debt, stockpiled enough food for a week's worth of lunches and dinners, splurged on this or that untasted ingredient or long-coveted piece of equipment, treated yourself to flowers and wine, and maybe even some new clothes. Finally—and *Mayflower Manners* says this without embarrassment or apology—you may even have done your soul some good. The ego may take pleasure in receiving, but the soul thrives mainly on giving.

And etiquette thrives on home entertainment. Hosting is the social act par excellence, and as such is dealt with in detail in all the usual references. Still, some new sorts of questions occur to one, such as . . .

WHO IS THAT LADY I SEE YOU WITH?

A friend is in town, and you invite him to your home for dinner—either at the last minute, to visit with you and your spouse, or with enough lead time to arrange a small party of six or eight. He accepts gladly, and then allows as how he will, during his trip to your city, be seeing a woman, whom he would like to bring along. You know, and he knows you know, and so forth, that **she is not his wife**.

May he bring her? Or would permitting that make you complicit in a crime? Is it wrong of him to ask? Does the fact that he is your guest oblige you to grant his request? Or, since you are the host, is it up to you?

For starters: He is wrong to ask. It places you in a difficult position—the very thing etiquette is designed to prevent. If he were traveling with his wife (or if he were not married, and seeing someone in your city), then his asking would be legitimate, and you would presumably (and should) invite her as well. This, though, is different.

Still, you've been asked. What to answer? It depends on your relationship with the man, and with his wife. If you know him socially, and therefore know her too, you are indeed being asked to collude in a "crime." It may not be your place to judge him (at least, to his face), but you are under no obligation to assist him, either. Your response, therefore, should be something on the order of "Oh, my, we were hoping to have you all to ourselves . . ." Whether or not he gets the message will depend on how attuned everyone is to the delicacy of the subject, and the corresponding significance of the subtext of what's being said. If he insists, you may become a little more explicit: "We'd love to see you. But perhaps you'd better keep that other relationship private."

If, on the other hand, your relationship is only with him (he is a colleague, a school chum, etc.), and you have no social contact with his wife, you may, *if you choose*, permit him to bring his friend. His reasons for doing so may be obscure, as much to himself as to you. (He may be in the process of provoking himself, semiconsciously, to end his marriage, for example.) But if you feel that it's not up to you to make those kinds of judgments, and that your loyalty to him as a friend outweighs other obligations, you may consent. (It's also arguable that at this stage, where friends are assisting each other in highly personal matters, where loyalty and confidences come into play, etiquette is irrelevant.)

Of course, you—or, perhaps more likely, your spouse—may be made uncomfortable by the whole matter. It might strike either or both of you as condoning a practice of which you disapprove. In that case, you may

reply with the comments noted above, expressing en-
thusiasm at seeing him but regret that his bringing a
companion would be inappropriate.

Someone will object that the above scenario is all but
unimaginable. Who would publicize (let alone jeopard-
ize) his secret out-of-town extramarital liaison by insisting
the partner be included at a dinner party? It does sound
unwise. But what is the twentieth century thus far, if
not ninety years during which the unimaginable has become the actual?

SEPARATION ANXIETY

"Love him/hate her," or vice versa, is a common refrain when discussing couples. People, unfortunately,
rarely bother to wonder whether their choice of mates
would be acceptable to friends and family. (And when
they do, often an answer in the negative seals the deal,
resulting in a wedding.) Whomsoever God has joined,
may a host issuing party invitations separate? **Is it possible to invite only one of a couple?**

First, it depends on the occasion. If it is a professional
one—an office party celebrating Christmas, a birthday,
etc.—then the host may invite whomever he or she
chooses, including an apologetic "no spouses" with the
invitation.

But you already knew that. The real problem arises
when the party is strictly social. Then it depends on the
couple. If they are married, they must both be invited
—and if one of the pair cannot attend, the other must
be encouraged to come alone. If they are living together,
you can try, but be prepared to be told that the two
partners "go everywhere" together, and to permit both

to come. If they are "seeing each other," then presumably your relationship is primarily (if not exclusively) with the person you wish to invite. If you really don't want him to bring his new girlfriend, you might try saying, "Oh, it's just some old friends. Why don't we meet Giselle another time?" But if he insists—which he ought not—you're stuck.

Note that much of this difficulty only applies when invitations are conveyed via phone calls—leading those being invited, reasonably enough, to suppose that the whole affair is somewhat informal and loose, and subject to improvisation. The way to formalize, and thus render more rigid, your invitation, is to do what you would probably do anyway for an affair of any size, scope, or level of fanciness, i.e., send a written invitation. It can be addressed to whomever you wish to invite, and can include "and guest" only when you mean it.

Not only does this announce unambiguously the terms of the invitation, but it offers you a way to avoid making allowances. When your single friend calls and asks if he can bring Giselle, you may say, distractedly, "Oh dear. Everything has been so carefully arranged . . . Can we meet her some other time?" The formality of the invitation hints at depths of complexity of which the poor fellow cannot be aware. You simply convey the impression that the whole project has a life of its own, the matter of the guest list is out of your hands, etc.

If, despite all this, he still insists, you are at a manners crossroads. If he says, "Either Giselle comes, or I shall be unable to attend," you will have to decide then and there whether to say, "Why, I had no idea your relationship with her had reached such a point. Of course she may come," or, "Oh, dear. I hope you will change your mind, but I'm afraid we'll have to see you some other time." He is being profoundly rude, and you'll have to intuit whether his attending with Giselle will put a fatal damper on the festivities, embarrass you and your spouse, or provide a (secretly) entertainingly appalling floor show and enough gossip fodder to fill a good hearty postmortem after they leave.

THE DISPLEASURE OF THEIR COMPANY
Now say you are a person of wide-ranging acquaintance. Among your friends there number several homosexuals, and some homophobes; various black people, and a few racists; sundry Jews, and a sprinkling of anti-Semites. **Can these less than compatible pairings be invited to the same party?**

Perhaps the real question is, Should they be? But suppose, for various reasons of social or professional obligation that really aren't too hard to imagine, they should. May they?

Of course, in each specific case the answer depends on the individual personalities. Many social and professional circles are replete with people of appalling prejudice who nonetheless are able to attend parties and dinners with perfect aplomb and flawless manners. (Washington, D.C. comes to mind.) Conversely, your specific friends (or, perhaps more likely, relatives) may be simply too volatile or argumentative to make inviting them to a party with people they are predisposed to dislike a good idea. As regards real personalities, only you know who is capable of socializing with whom without incident.

Theoretically, though, all this becomes a problem only

if one or both members of these matter/antimatter pairings is so rabid and uncontrollable as to make impossible their being brought together in one room. And, theoretically, you must assume that not to be the case. *Mayflower Manners* presumes everyone to be innocent until proven guilty, sane until proven mad, mannerly until proven rude, sober until proven drunk—and tolerant until proven bigoted. If the relevant personalities are such that you just don't know how well (or if at all) Uncle Harry will get along with your black neighbor from the apartment next door, invite both. In manners terms, you cannot be faulted.

In fact, you can be praised: If anything will get Uncle Harry to alter his view, it will be meeting a black person under the ideal circumstances of a party in your home. But apart from that, we must assume that everyone is an adult answerable to himself or herself. If, despite your assumption to the contrary, Uncle Harry insults your guest, you will as host of course apologize; but it will not be your "fault."

A TOOT AND A WHISTLE AND A
PLUNK AND A BOOM

One common cause of the sort of incompatibility among guests mentioned above is marriage: When spouses have different careers, their two distinct circles often intersect when they decide to entertain. He knows writers, she knows architects. He knows musicians, she lawyers. He knows doctors, she scientists. Usually this is a good thing; variety is the spice, not only of life, but of dinner.

But what if **her friends do drugs and his do not**? May drugs be used at such a mixed gathering?

First it is probably necessary to decide what we mean by "drugs." Twenty years ago, we would have meant literally anything from marijuana and hashish, on to Quaaludes and other "downers," through mescaline and LSD, to speed, cocaine, and various exotic substances like MDA and psilocybin. We would probably not have meant alcohol, PCP, or heroin; we would definitely not have meant crack. As for the legitimacy of their use in "mixed" company, the question would probably have not arisen. Twenty years ago, at least among the drug-doing community, etiquette was honored almost exclusively in the breach.

If someone had insisted on a ruling, it would probably have been: Do the drugs, so long as everybody has a chance to share. After all, the reasoning would have gone, traditional etiquette deems it polite to drink alcohol in the company of those who abstain, provided the function is avowedly social and the choice of the nondrinkers is respected. And isn't alcohol a "drug"? So the same applies to pot, acid, etc.

Of course, usually the only drug in question was one easily shared with a group—pot, hash, etc. Those individuals who, for example, dropped acid at a party without inviting others to join them were engaging in rude behavior, although that fact probably did not enter what remained of their consciousnesses at the time.

Today, after the smoked-out seventies and the coked-up eighties, the general view—or, at least, the general level of drug taking—is entirely different. Whether because of age, jadedness, the responsibilities of being parents, having to go to work the next day, or what, middle-class adults do fewer drugs, and far less frequently, than they used to. Almost all the exotic or psychedelic substances noted above have fallen into disfavor. Marijuana use is at a fraction of its former level. Even cocaine, formerly the drug of choice of adults between grad school and retirement age, has suffered opprobrium and rejection.

(Note that the same may not be true for *today's* college students, who have available to them almost as wide a range of illicit substances as their baby boomer counterparts did in the sixties. Certain species have died off or been replaced, e.g., MDA from days of yore seems to have been reincarnated, more or less, in "Ecstasy.")

But what of the general principle? May drugs be used at a party where half the assembled might decide to indulge, but the other half not?

It depends, as it so often used to, on the drug.

What is not permissible is a restricted access of one group to pleasures and fun not available to all. If the musicians, say, want to smoke marijuana, but the lawyers do not, the latter may simply decline politely when the joint—available to all—is passed. But if the lawyers wish to consume cocaine (which is not unimaginable), but the musicians do not (which, depending on the kind of musicians, sometimes *is* unimaginable), then either a sufficient quantity of the stuff must be available for everyone, or the host should discourage the whole idea.

Naturally, none of this addresses the legality, safety, cost, or social consquences of the use of whatever drug is at hand. Such matters are not etiquette's turf. *Mayflower Manners*, always up for a (polite) good time, prefers not to venture into territory where everyone, or even someone, has taken mind- or mood-altering chemicals.

GOSSIP

In General: Ah, gossip: the junk food of conversation, the cocaine of "interpersonal communication." It's bad for you, it's not nice, you feel slightly guilty—but everybody does it, and you want more.

As we enter the 1990s, the Era of Post-Gossip Gossip dawns. What began in the seventies with the Era of Low Gossip (*People* magazine; *Rolling Stone*), and reached maturity in the eighties with the Era of High Gossip (*Vanity Fair*; *Spy*), promises/threatens to attain new heights *and* new depths as we near the millennium. By the year 2000, computers will gossip for us; then, after we turn the machines off and go to bed, they will gossip *about* us. There will be gossip software (DishDirt, E-Z GABBER, TattleTale) and a cabinet-level Secretary of Gossip, Rumor, and Innuendo. A gossip columnist will win a Pulitzer Prize.

Or so it seems. Of all the changes in the relationships between men and women over the last thirty years, gossip may represent the most subtle yet one of the most pervasive. After all, up until the sixties, gossip was mainly something women did. Men, unfrivolously busy at work, traded "scuttlebutt" or, more officially, passed on rumors. It was women, the traditional guardians of hearth and home (i.e., of private life), who were "catty." As Lorenz Hart wrote about a certain lady, "she doesn't gossip/With the rest of the girls."

And boys, he could now add. As women have moved into the work force, become professionals, and asserted themselves sexually, so men have begun to cook, to change diapers, and to love gossip. College-educated fellows, who a generation ago would have turned their noses up at *Photoplay* or other movieland scandal sheets, now routinely read "Random Notes" (*Rolling Stone*), "People" (*Time*), "Newsmakers" (*Newsweek*), etc.

But if you're reading it in a magazine then it's really fake gossip, i.e., celebrity news. Another kind of fake gossip is social news, which concerns itself with the social lives of a city's aristocracy, of either the old money or nouveau riche persuasion. The principal medium for its dissemination is the "society" column in the local newspaper, with occasional augmentation courtesy of *Town & Country* or *Palm Beach Life*. Events suitable for reporting include charity fetes and balls, benefit banquets, deb parties, dinner parties, cocktail receptions, weddings, and so on—wherever a man can wear a tuxedo without being one of the "help."

It should be remembered that most items in a newspaper societal column find their way there with the help, if not at the request, of the event's host or hostess. Persons eager to advance their social standing will invite the columnist (but settle, if need be, for one of her or his "very social" friends, i.e., stringers). Many will even retain the services of a public relations firm to distribute guest lists, menus, floral decoration details, gown descriptions, designer names, etc. Such social butterflies—or does one mean killer bees?—will actively court influential columnists, inviting them on yacht trips, country weekends, and so forth.

This is gossip-as-PR-handout. *Mayflower Manners* prefers to leave discussion of such immodesty and calculation to others. Instead, it will concentrate on good honest working-stiff gossip, the kind of dirt dishing that goes on between consenting adults about other adults who, were they present, would probably not be so consenting.

THE BIG QUESTION
Is it bad manners to gossip?

This question, which on the surface is bad enough— it threatens to rob us of all that fun—is in fact more complicated than it appears. It is not bad manners to do something "to" someone with whom you are not actually interacting.

However, what is not bad manners may in fact be "bad morals." Not that anyone asked, but **is it immoral to gossip about someone?** Don't pretend this isn't a good question. The very way we describe and talk about gossip, the whole atmosphere in which it is conveyed, suggests something wicked or forbidden. "Don't tell anyone I told you this," we start out, or "You didn't hear this from me, but—"

Real gossip is the exposure of other people's secrets, facts they either don't want others to know or don't want others to know *yet*. The bigger the secret, the more potent the item. Really big secrets are those that involve breaking societal taboos—i.e., taboos that apply to the gossips as well as their subject. Unfortunately for contemporary gossips, many of the topics that used to provide surefire fodder for gossip have today lost their luster. Formerly secret, scandalous subjects such as alcoholism, venereal disease, homosexuality, childbirth out of wedlock, drug addiction, etc., have become "societal problems." Yesterday's hot gossip is today's "Donahue."

Real gossip is a violation of someone's privacy. Hence the aura of sinfulness that always accompanies it.

Sinful, okay—but is it immoral? Certainly it is, if you willfully repeat a statement about someone which you know to be false, for the purpose either of harming his reputation, manipulating a third party, or of sharing a scandalized thrill with the people you're talking to. That's gossiping-as-lying. As for repeating something that you know *might* (or might not) be true, but whose truth you can't (or choose not to) confirm . . . that's the sort of smear-by-innuendo that takes place in politics all the time. Will you think *Mayflower Manners* a big drag (or, worse, unworldly) if it suggests that this, too, is immoral?

In any case, moral or im-, gossiping is not nice. That's why it's the kind of fun that it is. Where not-niceness fits on a scale of morality is for everyone to decide for himself.

AND YOU, MADAME, ARE NO GENTLEMAN

Having suggested that gossip was originally a woman's pastime, one wonders: Might it still be, secretly? Meaning: **Does sex matter?** If a man punches an individual in the nose, our judgment of that act depends in part on whether or not that individual is a woman. Does the same hold when a man gossips about an individual? Is it somehow bad, for example, if a man gossips with a group of women? What about the entire list of possible combinations and permutations?

ANATOMY OF GOSSIP: GENDER COMPONENTS

1. A man gossips about a woman, with a group of women.

2. A woman gossips about a man, with a group of men.

3. A man gossips about a woman, with a group of men.

4. A woman gossips about a man, with a group of women.

5. A man gossips about a man, with a group of men.

6. A woman gossips about a woman, with a group of women.

7. A man gossips about a man, with a group of women.

8. A woman gossips about a woman, with a group of men.

9. Men and women all gossip about each other in a group.

Isn't this exhausting? Fortunately, the answer to all is, in the words of one source, "gossip transcends gender." Men to women, women to men—what matters, in the etiquette of gossip, is what is being said, not who is saying it or to whom.

A MAN, A PLAN, A CANARD

You are present when a bit of gossip is presented which **you know to be untrue**. Everyone else—the "primary source," and his audience—believes it to be factual. **Is it bad manners for you to defend the subject of the**

gossip, to correct the primary source, and announce the truth? Or is it inappropriately chivalric, totally party-poopish, or something equally uncool?

Even though your doing so may deflate the ballooning delight of the assembled, you should—diplomatically, so as not to insult the primary source—explain that the item is untrue. This whether the subject is a friend or not, but especially if he is a friend. Taking part in gossip may be good clean—well, good dirty—fun, but being party to a lie is something else.

One source went so far as to state that you should refute gossip about a friend even if it *is* true. That seems risky—what you accomplish as a loyal friend may end up costing you in terms of your own credibility. However, you can, in those situations, downplay the negative gossip and try to change the subject by bringing up positive things about your much-discussed friend.

TINKER, TAILOR, SOLDIER, MOLE

Having witnessed others gossiping about your poor friend, you now wonder: **Should you tell him?** If the gossips are also friends of yours, would that constitute treason? Is gossip inherently off-the-record (i.e., are all present automatically sworn to secrecy), or only if so specified at the time?

This question is less about your behavior toward the gossips than about you and your friend. If the gossip deals with things over which your friend has little or no control (a tic, a scandalous parent or spouse), telling him would not accomplish much and probably be hurtful. However, if your friend believes those gossiping about him to be friends, but in fact they are not, your friend ought to know it.

As to what is on or off the record, there is no point in being disingenuous: Even if no one says, "This is between us," everyone who gossips believes that those taking part will maintain security and respect the confidential nature of the "information." Nonetheless, it may well be that your loyalty to your friend outweighs your loyalty to a group of people willing to say unkind things about him behind his back. You may, though, when telling him, take steps (i.e., swear *him* to secrecy) to assure that the gossipers don't learn who revealed their identities.

Of course, it never hurts to tell someone if the gossip about him was good. But how often does that happen?

THE WHOLE TRUTH

Now the gang is gossiping away about a subject on which you happen to be well informed. All eyes turn toward you, and **someone urges you to add what you know. Must you?** If, for whatever reason, you prefer not to, may you lie—claim ignorance, say you weren't there? And if the reason for your reticence is a **promise you made to X not to tell, while those all around you seem to know all about the thing you've sworn to keep secret, can you just plunge in and gab,** on the assumption that the promise to X is now obsolete?

While gossip can be thrilling, and creates a momentum of its own, you are under no obligation to add to it. Rather than lie, however, and risk your future credibility, you should either temporize—try to shift the subject, deny

knowing tangential things of which you really are igno-
rant, etc.—or, if all else fails, politely decline to comment. Act modest about it (instead of self-righteous),
and those present may be impressed with your discretion,
rewarding you with fabulous tidbits later on.

As for discussing the thing you promised X you would
keep secret, most sources agreed that you are free to
discuss it so long as everyone else is, but you should not
chip in any new material the others may not be aware of.

DID YOU MAKE THE ENEMIES LIST?
**Having told your friend that she was the subject of
gossip, should you also tell her by whom?**

Only if you can be sure she will not somehow reveal
that you were the source of her knowing. You might want
to be a saint, but you don't have to be a martyr.

WELCOME TO THE CLUB, MAYBE
As to that group . . .

Some have suggested that **in order to be "admitted"
to a gossiping group, one must add a new item of
one's own** about the subject at hand. Must one?

The answer, as it so often is, is "No, but—" The
"but" points to the true purpose of gossip, which is not
(claims of the scandal sheet press notwithstanding) to
"spread information" or serve "the public's right to know."
The true purpose of gossip is to have a cheap thrill hearing about the misfortune of others (be it real, potential,
impending, or imaginary), and enjoying the fact that it
isn't happening to oneself.

Therefore, while new members of the group will always be welcome if they present a fresh item at the door,

all that's really needed is something to heighten everyone else's Level of Titillation. And all that takes is an expression or comment that emphasizes the titillating aspect of whatever is already under discussion. Phrases like "You're kidding!" and "I don't believe it!" and "That can't possibly be true!" serve this purpose admirably.

AS THE WORM TURNS

And now, alas, **you are the subject, and X is the friend who has told you** that A, B, and C—with whom you shared countless hours of glee dishing everyone else on earth—have been talking about you. **If confronting them would reveal X as your source, should you do so anyway? If not, then what?**

If the gossip is untrue, you have the right to set the record straight. Bear in mind, though, that if doing so would compromise X, you would be in the untenable position of showing X less loyalty than he showed you —after all, he could as easily not have told you that you were being talked about. If you can speak up without compromising him, do so.

But if you can't, you shouldn't. (Yes, it will rankle; console yourself by asking, What good would it do? A would deny it, B would say you misunderstood, and C would tell you to come off it, that he who lives by the dish dies by the dish.) Instead, inscribe their treachery in letters of fire on your brain (i.e., remember this), and never trust them again. Which doesn't mean never *gossip* with them again, thank God.

STOOL PIGEONS COME HOME TO ROOST

From the above unfortunate scenario: you do confront

the gossips. Even if they don't know how you found out, **should the person who told you (X) go to them and apologize—for, in effect, "finking" on the group?**

Unless he has betrayed a promise not to reveal who said what about whom, X is under no obligation to apologize to the group. Gossiping is a public act; for people who have been bandying details of another person's life to complain that their privacy has been violated seems a bit much.

Of course, the group may deduce that X was the leak, and withdraw their trust from him accordingly. But that's another matter, and a risk X takes in telling his friend (you) about the group.

FYD (FOR YOUR DISINFORMATION)

Having gossiped your brains out all the previous night, or week, or month, **you now discover that some unpleasant item you have been spreading** (yes, it *does* sound like a disease) **is untrue.** What, if anything, should you do? Contact those you told and set the record straight? Notify the subject and apologize? Take an oath never to gossip again?

Amusingly, sources' answers came in three parts:

1. By Jove, yes, contact as many people as you can and correct the misapprehension you have unfortunately helped foster.

2. Well, hold on. Unless one was oneself in danger of being exposed as a spreader of false gossip, maybe it would be best to just let the matter drop . . .

3. But in no case notify the subject.

For once, *Mayflower Manners* wishes to take a slight issue with its otherwise impeccable sources. If the item you have been erroneously spreading is important—especially to its subject—you should make an effort to contact those with whom you gossiped and set the record straight. The only thing worse than being caught doing something scandalous is being unjustly accused of it.

FACE TO FACE, OR A FACE
IN THE CROWD?

You are with a small group of people, and hear a tasty story. **Do you have an inherent "right" to repeat it to others? What if you are asked by the group not to? And is the situation any different if you hear the story from one other person during a tête-à-tête? If the other person makes you swear not to repeat it, do you really have to honor the pledge?** Or does gossip consist of secrets that no one is expected to keep? (After all, your friend just told *you*, didn't he?) **And if you do spread the story, was your pledge a lie? How much does gossip "count" on one's "permanent record" of honor?**

Whew! First things first. Like sex, gossip acquires a different character when it is pursued in a group. As one source put it, "no one gives intimate gossip to a group of people," while "a one-on-one is a much more sacred exchange, especially if they're a good friend."

Which is to say, sources did not so much feel they had a "right" to repeat things heard in a group as they saw no reason not to, considering the nature of the things one in fact ends up hearing en masse. As to being asked not to repeat an item, most said their honoring of that request would depend on the kind of gossip it was, and their relationship with its subject.

This is not altogether defensible, although there is some sense to the notion that if you're telling so many people this item, it can't be all that sensitive. Another source captured the . . . *flexibility* of this kind of standard, when he introduced a bit of gossip with the caveat "Don't tell anyone . . . Well, tell everyone, but tell *them* not to tell anyone."

Promising a single individual, however, has a much more binding effect, particularly if he is a close friend. Even then, though, an item meant for your ears only should be so stipulated. After all, all gossips know what pleasure they get from unveiling juicy items; they should therefore bear in mind that unless specifically compelled not to, others will look forward to the same pleasure when passing the story along.

Gossip is thus not so much "a secret no one is expected to keep" as a kind of classified information circulating through a community capable of revising not only its own security clearances, but the classification of the information itself. How much taking part in that process "counts" with regard to one's honor is a function of who is harmed, or whose trust is betrayed, by its dissemination—effects not always easy, or even possible, to calculate.

Of course, your honor never suffers if you keep your mouth shut and say nothing, but what fun is that?

ANTE UP

You find yourself chatting with a group of gossipers, each of whom contributes a delectable morsel about Z. It occurs to you that you have an item no one else does. **After everyone else has revealed his or her story, is**

it wrong of you—for whatever reason—to hold back
and decline to reveal yours?

In conflict here is your obligation to the group versus
your obligation to someone else—to Z, or to X, the person who provided you with your item, and so on. On
such occasions, personal relationships take priority over
group obligations. Did you promise X never to repeat it?
Will it get Z in trouble? Is it a significantly more personal,
intimate, or damaging item than what the others have
shared? In all such cases, your silence is appropriate.

SHE WHO DIGGETH THE PIT ...

Giselle, that catty thing, is a **world-class gossip**. Now
she hears from . . . well, someone . . . that **people are
saying such-and-such about her. Is it hypocritical of
her to take offense**, to seek out those people and de-
nounce them?

It is not hypocritical, and is quite appopriate, if the
gossip is untrue. This, of course, assuming she deals only
in the most scrupulously factual gossip herself.

PHONING IT IN
How to Call in an Item to a Gossip Columnist

Not that you want to, of course. Who cares about
celebrities? Still, in certain places (New York, Los
Angeles, Washington, D.C.) celebrity spotting is like
bird watching: often tedious, sometimes exciting, you
do it at your own pace, and it gets you out of the
house. And while there is some private satisfaction to
be had from knowing you've seen prime-time heart-
throb David Hunk and his wife, Kimerlee, indulging

in a fistfight in front of Le Côte du Paint, it seems to mean so much more, and to feel more real, to record the sighting. Here, for aspiring celebrity Audubons, are some tips:

1. Most columnists prefer to work from printed material, either a professional press release or at least a typed-up version of the story. Columnists with a good personal relationship with the caller will usually take a really juicy item over the phone, even if it features celebrities the caller does not know personally. Otherwise, the credibility and acceptability of the item depends on the caller's relationship with the subject of the story, and what one columnist called "the gravity of the dirt."

2. Information must be "exclusive" (*never* phone the same item to more than one columnist), fact-checked, and pertinent to the columnist's area of reporting. (That is, some write about society, others about the entertainment industry.)

3. Three types of items submitted to a columnist:

(a) A "free item" is one you pass along to a columnist with whom you either do have a relationship or do not. The more credible you have proven in the past, obviously, the more the writer is likely to believe you in the present.

(b) A "pay item" fetches approximately a hundred dollars, and is submitted, typewritten, to a national columnist. It must be exclusive and checkable/verifiable. Magazines like *People* will often pay what one source called "substantial money" for a major scoop, but it must never have been published before, be completely true, and be easily fact-checked and verifiable.

(c) A "trade-off item" is one which a publicist will exchange for a plug (i.e., for a client) at a later date.

WRITING IT UP
Basic Facts About Gossip Columnists

There is an etiquette to being, and interacting with, a gossip columnist. Begin with the fact mentioned above, i.e., that a columnist is always invited to a party or an event because its host wants the event mentioned in the newspaper. Columnists, therefore, are always on duty. If you have invited one, it is only fair to warn any celebrities that may be unfamiliar with the local columnists. It is a nice gesture if guests at the party also tip off the unsuspecting celeb.

In fact, one source stated that a columnist has a responsibility to let those present know "who he is," by, say, prominently displaying a pad and pen.

Another source claims that it is not fair to say to a columnist, in such a situation, that your words or behavior are "off the record." For one thing, while for everyone else the event is at least partially social (i.e., private), for the columnist it is purely professional. For another, columnists are often beset with claims of "this is off the record" by people whom the writers would never bother to put *on* the record. This kind of relentless grandiosity and egotism gets annoying, even for showbiz columnists who usually thrive on it.

(It's bearable when the grandiose egotist is a star, not so bearable when he or she isn't.)

As for what a columnist will not print, and how it is checked: Dailies rarely check, as they don't have the time, and therefore depend mainly on trusted sources. Most items from unknown sources, if they cannot be confirmed, will not be printed. Magazines are much more meticulous about fact checking, and will usually seek verification from a second and third party before running a story.

It is rare to see a columnist or magazine print something that would truly hurt someone, or that is particularly vicious—*except*. Except, that is, in the case of people whose lifestyle or past deeds have given rise to a general feeling that "they deserve it." Yes, this is purely subjective; its exercise is one of the things that makes one magazine different from another.

American libel laws make it hard to win a judgment against a publication that prints something untrue. Among other things, you as plaintiff have to prove it is *not* true. The paper or magazine does not have to provie that it *is* true.

Finally, one source stated that a gossip columnist has a duty to be factual but not a right to be judgmental. And another mentioned the concept of karma: everything you do or say (or write) will come back to you.

UNTRUTH OR UNCONSEQUENCES

Here's a sticky one: You hear an item of gossip that is simultaneously too juicy not to repeat and too improbable or terrible to be believed. In fact, **you don't believe it. Can you still pass it along, if you preface it with a disclaimer** such as "I really don't believe this, but I heard that—"?

If it's trivial, announce the disclaimer, and then get on with it. If all in attendance react with (a) complete credulity and (b) a willingness to give you credit for the item, be sure you impress upon them that you don't believe it, it's only a rumor, etc. Otherwise, if it proves false, they'll think you responsible for either a deliberate untruth or a poorly considered nugget of fool's gold. Worse: if it has damaging consequences, and its subject wants to know who spread the rumor, all fingers will point to you.

If it's really ugly or hurtful, then—in the succinct words of one source—"shut up."

THE WHOLE HALF-TRUTH, AND NOTHING BUT THE HALF-TRUTH

Finally, this party-pooping bit of rumination:

What *is* gossip? Is it like ordinary conversation, in which only calculating people knowingly tell lies? Or is it a fantasy exercise, in which everyone is allowed to speculate, exaggerate, and play fast and loose with the facts? Or is it a sort of socially condoned form of illegality, the conversational equivalent of smoking marijuana or driving over 55?

Actually, this is where all the ethical and semiethical considerations give way to actual etiquette, because your way of answering this question has bearing on how you interact with others and how others regard you.

The whole raison d'être of gossip is that it *is* truth—

secret truth, the real truth, ultra-truth, truth on stilts. Hence its power to do damage when it is inaccurate. And, therefore, hence the gossip's responsibility to be fair, truthful, and careful about what he or she disseminates.

A gossip heard by others to spread cruel, ugly, or hurtful things—or patently untrue things—will be seen by his audience as being . . . well, cruel, ugly, and hurtful. (Unless the audience is the same.) Ethics aside, such gossip places its listeners in an uncomfortable position. The more gleefully a gossip shares a nasty item, the more he is seen to use emotional extortion, forcing his audience to share his pleasure at the misfortune of others.

Which is not to say that *Mayflower Manners* is above enjoying hearing the odd bit of negative gossip from time to time. But it draws the line at gossip that would inflict pain or otherwise damage someone's life.

This is doubly true for printed gossip, which has a far greater capacity to hurt than does the spoken kind. (Most people think—wrongly—that "they couldn't print that stuff if it wasn't true.") Matters concerning sex, drugs, and state of health must be handled with special care, lest people's lives be destroyed.

In any sort of quality company, people judge the teller of gossip just as much as they judge its subject.

$\mathcal{T}$ELEPHONE

In General: $\mathcal{W}$ith the increasing sophistication of telephone equipment comes a number of new and hitherto unknown ways in which to offend people. That is the consequences of any new technology, of course, but the telephone is a special case. There is something so ambiguous about the phone. We have direct contact with another. We can even hear him breathing (sometimes, alas, that's all we hear). But we cannot see him. In fact, we must take it on faith that the person speaking to us is himself. And even if the primary message he conveys is clear and comprehensible—e.g., "Of course I love you"—we have, literally, only his word for it. All the other cues we habitually look for in order to gauge a person's statement—his facial expressions, whether he makes enough (or too much) eye contact, his "body language"—are denied us.

An elaborate protocol for the phone has developed over the decades. Add to this the technical advances of the last ten years—answering machines, Call Waiting, Direct Dial Long Distance, etc.—and the result is a plethora of new and exciting opportunities for men and women alike to do the wrong thing. Time was when telephone etiquette was not much different from interpersonal etiquette: You said hello, asked with a "please" and responded with a "thank you," spoke clearly, and wondered whether or not to correct someone who mispronounced your name.

Now, though, things are more complicated. We use

the phone for everything from meeting strangers to ordering dinner. And when we happen not to be at home, and are unable to use the instrument, there are any number of machines we can buy which will be "happy" to use it on our behalf.

Thus the need for a more comprehensive telephone etiquette: What follows makes no claim at being exhaustive. From being left to die on the vine of Call Waiting, to having to shout to a caller on a speakerphone in a *car*, there will always be a new way to insult and be insulted. But it does offer a few suggestions about some common vexations.

MANY ARE CALLED

Begin with the simple matter of phoning someone who, either at work or at home, is on another line. Having reached either the person or his/her secretary, you know that he or she is in. And you know that they know you have called. **Who calls whom back?**

Usually, of course, he is obliged to return your call. (Not that everyone does, of course. Inaccessibility is a hallmark of power, and not calling back is one of the more Zen-like ways of asserting yourself.) If, however, you have called this person to ask a favor, you would be wise to volunteer to do the calling back.

This is canny for three reasons. One is, it sounds (and is) a bit deferential, which is an attitude you might wish to cultivate when asking someone to do you a service. Second, it spares you the time and energy of waiting by the phone, wondering when the person ever will call back. It also shields you from the occasional slow, withering death of a part of your self-esteem when it gradually dawns on you that he *isn't* calling back. Third, when you do get through, you have built up some momentum rather than passively sitting there like an unpopular high school student waiting to be asked to the prom. Even though your need to ask a favor places you in an "inferior" position, by returning the call yourself you seize the initiative.

Only the first of these pertain strictly to etiquette, but the mannerly thing to do often proves to be the strategically smart thing to do. But now suppose Ed calls you when you are out. You receive the message, and **call him back. He's not in**, there is no secretary or machine, etc. In other words, he has no way to know you've tried to reach him. Who owes whom the call now? You've tried, and he's out. Have you done your bit? Or should you try a few more times before leaving it up to him?

In fact, you should try two or three more times. Just as it wasn't your "fault" that he called when you were not available, so it isn't his fault that he's out when you called back. Such situations are scored on a balance sheet of awareness. Thus far, both of you are aware that he's tried you, but only one of you (i.e., you) is aware that you've reciprocated. After two or three more tries, you may conclude that you'll never know when he'll be back, and besides, by then you've left enough time for *him* to know that he himself has been out long enough for you to have tried and failed to have reached him.

Clear? Oh dear. Well, try reading it again. But now suppose you know that he uses a **beeper**. Is there **a good or bad time to have him beeped?**

Ownership of a beeper should not be construed by others as signalling a willingness to answer any call, twenty-

four hours a day. Think of the beeper as another extension of the standard phone, and call it during standard
hours (for which, see below).

SPEAKING, OR SHUTTING, UP

What if, after asking for Miss Person, you experience the
following **aggravating exchange:**

YOU: Is this Miss Person's office?

SHE: Yes.

YOU (after brief puzzled pause): Is Miss Person in,
please?

SHE: Yes.

YOU: (after longer, more irrational pause): May I speak
with her, please?

SHE: Yes.

YOU (after supremely long pause of maximum annoyance): Is this she?

SHE: Yes.

The central question—What do such people think they
are doing when they play cat-and-mouse like this on a
perfectly legitimate business call?—is outside the scope
of this book. The next question—What do I do and
say?—will occasion an answer that won't be as disappointing as it may look at first.

What you crave to say, of course, is, "Why didn't you
say so in the first place, you idiot?" Don't. Few things
constitute as severe a breach of etiquette as calling someone an idiot—not because etiquette is a system of rules
designed to prevent you from doing or saying what you

really want to other people, but because it is one of several systems of rules designed to prevent other people from doing or saying what they really want to you. And, considering that there is only one of you, and more than four billion other people, it could be agreed that this seems like a good deal.

However, etiquette, like every other elaborate system devised by civilization to create order, contains within itself certain loopholes through which the adept may occasionally scramble. One is that you may express your true feelings in certain instances, provided you do so in a form that is outwardly courteous and deferential. Therefore, when the infuriating Miss Person has sprung on you the startling news that she is herself, and continues to be irritatingly dilatory in holding up her end of the conversation, you should proceed briskly and cut your losses.

Or, you might try raising your voice just a little, and saying—not shouting, but saying firmly—"Hello? Miss Person? Can't you hear me?" Either she will say yes, or she will not. (With this woman, who really knows?) In any case, after a second's pause, say loudly, "I'm afraid we must have a bad connection. You seemed not to have heard me ask for you. I'll hang up and call back." Either she will protest that that is unnecessary, or she will not. Give her a moment to begin, then hang up, wait a few minutes (to allow her, ideally, to think about it), and then try again.

True, the extra call means extra expense. But the alternative is to call her an idiot. What is money, when etiquette is at stake?

TIME AND AGAIN AND AGAIN

The wonderful, and yet also horrible, thing about the telephone is that through it, we are accessible to everyone, all the time. (This unless we have an unlisted number, in which case we are accessible to everyone who knows the number, all the time.) But then, they are accessible to us, too, and sometimes we are tempted to take advantage of that fact. And while we might not ordinarily phone friends past a certain time—say, 9 P.M.—we might decide to call people who "work for" us, i.e., professionals. After all, we're paying, aren't we?

But professionals, even though they carry their office "with" them (in the sense that they are able at least to consult no matter where they are), are entitled to time during which business calls ought not to come. **Phoning professionals** should take place between 9 A.M. and 6 P.M., with allowances made for two kinds of exceptions. One is if a significant difference in time zones requires taking liberties with those hours (but see the chart below for a sense of who, at various places around the world, might be doing what at a given time). The other is, of course, in a case of emergency.

Obviously, the kind of emergency to occasion a call will depend on the kind of professional answering the phone. Plumbers and mob hit men have jobs which invite erratically timed calls, and in such cases (especially the latter) you should inquire as to which hours are absolutely forbidden. Then there is the case of obstetricians, perhaps the last remaining sort of doctors willing to get out of bed and go to work in response to an off-hours call. Their numbers are dwindling so quickly these days, especially away from the larger urban areas, that those women finding themselves in need of obstetrical services late at night are probably better off calling a mob hit man.

As for those **widely separated time zones**, the best advice one can give in making calls across them is, Show restraint and hope for understanding. One source mentioned the case of a literary agent in London who, eager at ten o'clock one morning to speak to an American colleague, phoned her up at her apartment. This in itself was not unusual; the time differential between the London and New York offices made calling agents at home a common practice. Unfortunately, the gentleman forgot to do the necessary calculations. He woke his American counterpart at 4 A.M. Their conversation, apparently, was brief, and probably not that "literary."

It's easy to forget that lunchtime in Philadelphia is Happy Hour in Milan. Note the disorienting facts on the chart below.

The chart makes it clear why the goal of world peace is so elusive: No one is available long enough, at the same time, to reach an agreement on it. Just as half the world is taking its seat and preparing to talk terms, the other half is calling for the dinner check and getting ready to hit the hay. Therefore, when phoning area codes not immediately adjacent to your own, check the time zones and do the arithmetic. If you foresee making such calls in the future, check with the other party as to what times are good, or, at least, less bad, for you to phone. But certainly no one should be called at his home after 9 P.M. Which means, readers who live on America's West Coast, that you have until 1 P.M. to call Europe. And your calls to Japan must be made not long after 4 A.M.(!)

WHO'S DOING WHAT WHEN

Comparison of Activities During Ultra-Long-Distance Phone Calls

Where caller lives	Caller's time	What caller is probably doing	Where callee lives	Callee's time	What callee is probably doing
N.Y.	9 A.M.	Starting work	L.A.	6 A.M.	Waking up
S.F.	10 A.M.	Hitting stride	Boston	1 P.M.	Eating lunch
Chicago	12 P.M.	Thinking about lunch	London	6 P.M.	Predinner drink
Houston	1 P.M.	Eating lunch	Tokyo	4 A.M.	Sleeping
Osaka	12 P.M.	Thinking about lunch	Atlanta	10 P.M.	Sleeping
Moscow	3 P.M.	Falling asleep at desk	D.C.	7 A.M.	Getting up
D.C.	4 P.M.	Sleeping at desk	Moscow	12 A.M.	Sleeping in bed

So much for business. Are there **permissible hours for personal calls,** both during the week and on weekends and holidays? Of course. In general, personal calls should not come before 9 A.M. nor after 9 P.M. Naturally, there will be exceptions: urgent news, late-breaking stock tips, babysitters canceling at 7 A.M. on the morning you have an appointment at 8 A.M., etc. These, by definition, are exempt from the rule. But otherwise the rationale for such times goes thus: The 9 A.M. time lets people feed and get out the door those they must (which sometimes includes themselves), while the 9 P.M. limit allows them to enjoy a quiet—or, at least, private—domestic interlude after dinner, free of the necessity to leap up from book, bath, TV, kids, or bed to answer the phone. Single people may be called until 10 P.M.

Of course, it goes without saying that any phone calls received **during dinner** should be returned after the meal is complete.

YOU'VE REALLY GOTTA ME ON HOLD
Being put on Hold is a little like being put *in* a hold, i.e., the hold of a ship, where it's dark and lonely, and where the only form of entertainment is to strain to hear various telltale sounds that might offer a clue as to when you will be released. In the telephonic equivalent of hold, of course, there is often another form of entertainment—music—about which see below.

Of all the abuses to which users of the telephone are subject, Hold is perhaps the most aggravating. One reason for this may be because having grown accustomed to immediate results whenever we use the phone (even if we get a wrong number, we get it *fast*), the netherworld of Hold can be a place where time stands still, where we may wait a moment or an eternity—indeed, where a moment *is* an eternity. All control has been gently (or, more often, rudely) taken from our hands, and we are at the mercy, not even of the person we've called, but usually of his or her assistant, receptionist, etc.—a stranger, whose interest in rescuing us from Hold lessens with every other caller who "joins" us there.

Nonetheless, anyone worth calling will have Hold, and will put us there sooner or later. This is even true, increasingly, for private phone lines: Call Waiting is a sort of mini-Hold and, like a mini-hold on a ship, is even more cramped and uncomfortable and dreary than the real thing.

There are some who might be tempted to regard **Hold as a metaphor for the human condition.** But such an attitude, perhaps understandably, confuses *Mayflower Manners* with Samuel Beckett. Calling someone up, getting their answering machine, listening to their message, frantically conceiving your own message, and then waiting for a beep that never comes: *That* is a *Mayflower Manners* metaphor for the human condition.

As for Hold, a word in its defense: Being put on Hold is not necessarily rude, depending on **how you are put there, and how long you are made to stay.**

You should be put there with courtesy and deference. While it is true that often the conditions which require a receptionist to place you on Hold—i.e., many callers to deal with—are the very ones that might provoke a receptionist to behave badly, nonetheless: Polite is polite. The person answering the phone should greet you with the name of the company or firm, and either pause to let you state your business or, in especially frenzied situations, prepare to put you on what might be called Peremptory Hold. Not having time to inquire as to your business, she instead (let's assume the receptionist is a woman) will ask, "Would you mind if I put you on Hold for a moment? Thank you." She should then not immediately flick you into oblivion, leaving you graciously murmuring, "Not at all" to yourself. Instead, she should pause for your reply, the only permissible one being "Not at all." Of course, it is not true. Of course you mind. She probably minds having to answer your call. What is relevant here is courtesy, not truth.

If placed on Peremptory Hold, you should be retrieved from it and sped on your telephonic way in no more than fifteen seconds. If, on the other hand, she has had the time (and courtesy) to ask to whom you wish to speak, you ought to wait at least thirty seconds on Hold before starting to fume. Through no fault of her own, she may be having trouble getting through to the person you're calling.

What should you **listen to while on Hold**? How, out of the immense range of auditory entertainments available to modern man, from classical and popular music, to talk shows, to business shows, to Broadway hits, drama, comedy routines, inspirational messages, and ecumenical discussions, can a company know what to program for the enjoyment of those whom it keeps waiting? The answer is surprisingly simple: You should listen to nothing.

Companies which provide privately programmed taped selections, or commercial radio broadcasts, should discontinue this practice immediately. If being on Hold is a little like being in solitary confinement, being on Hold and having to listen to something—anything—is like being in solitary confinement in a straitjacket. A person is trapped: He cannot jot notes, or skim reading material, or chat with a visitor, or meditate on his philosophy of life, or anything else, while that music (or, worse, commercial) is playing in his earpiece. And he cannot put the handset down until someone gets back on the line, because he runs the risk of not hearing their return. This principle is so simple, so self-evident, and so frequently violated, it makes one despair of American business ever catching up to anybody, let alone its more insightful competitors.

DOING IT IN PUBLIC

With the breakup of AT&T, mystery brands of **pay phones** have proliferated; fortunately, this is neither the time nor the place to discuss their offputting appearance, their irritating lack of access to many long distance services, their usurious rates, the heartfelt emotions we experience when they take our money and then fail to work, etc.

No, the real question is, **Must I hurry up when using a pay phone** for which other people are waiting? And, conversely, if I see someone using the only pay phone in sight (or the only one that works) who is dawdling, or giggling, or speaking in some other equally frivolous manner, while I (obviously) wait and snort and conspicuously check my watch, do I have the right to get mad?

Pay phones, like almost everything else in the world, inspire two schools of thought. One holds that since you're paying, and you were there first, you're entitled to take your own sweet time. The other view, of course, is that when using a public convenience for which others are waiting, you act as efficiently as possible and let the next guy have a turn.

Both arguments have their flaws. The quarter you put in the phone does not buy you permission to monopolize a public facility, only to use it. On the other hand, where there is one pay phone, there are usually others. In the case of a city street, the others can be several blocks away, but they are nonetheless accessible. Why should I cut short my conversation because you are indisposed to walk one or two blocks?

Worse, a phone call is not—unlike, say, a cab ride— the sort of service that can be clearly defined. Any but the most brief calls of inquiry ("What time does the feature start?" e.g.), involves general atmospheric chit-chat, buttering up, letting oneself be flattered, polite questions about the family, etc. How, then, can we hope to define when a call "should" be over?

This is a debate for which lawyers are well-suited and highly paid, but for which *Mayflower Manners*, though equally suited, is less appropriately compensated. Let us therefore cut it short with the admonition—or plea, actually —to seek a workable medium between telephonic necessity and civic responsibility. If you are on the only phone in sight, and someone else is waiting, you should ask the person on the other end of the line to wait a moment, and inquire as to whether the next caller is in a hurry or not. Tell him whether you intend to be one minute or twenty. If he's willing to wait, fine—but then you must take only as long as you said you would, and not exploit his patience. If he is not willing to wait, you may either suggest he use the next nearest phone (assuming you know where it is, and tell him), or you may wrap up your business and bring your call to an end. If, after deferring thus to him, you discover that there is only the one phone, and he is willing to wait one minute but not twenty, you may take five, prefacing it with "I'll be as fast as I can."

After such a conundrum, it's a relief to turn to something easy, such as **tearing pages out of public phone books**. People do so in order to remember—or, rather, *instead* of trying to remember—phone numbers, addresses, etc. Is it permissible? No. Yes, Jack Nicholson looked great rippling out that page of the county real estate register in *Chinatown*. But (a) that was in California, and (b) it was a movie.

As for the individual **calling from a noisy pay phone**: His choice of telephone may have the paradoxical effect of forcing *the other* person to speak up or yell in order to be heard—in which case he should apologize. The callee, in turn, should be prepared to speak up or yell, and assume that the caller did not deliberately choose a phone booth along the flight path of a convoy of cement trucks.

THE BEEP GOES ON: ANSWERING MACHINES AND SERVICES

The advent of the telephone answering machine has heralded not only a new age in automatic message-taking and message-leaving, but in selective call-avoiding and caller-fooling. Like most technological blessings, this one is mixed. Yes, one would like to be able to choose to be "home to" some callers and not to others. And how simple it is to hover over the machine, listening in with impunity as X (whom we would rather not speak to at the moment, thank you) leaves his/her message and remains unaware of our presence. But at such times we do not get off scot-free. Now X knows that we know that he/she called. Or, we will know, as soon as we "get home." And thereafter we have no excuse, other than an increasingly feeble "the machine didn't work," for not calling back.

The alternative? (a) Take the phone off the hook—and risk missing calls from people we do wish to speak to; (b) have no machine—and forfeit getting messages when we actually are away; or (c) use an answering service. Then, when X tells us he left a message with the service three days ago, and asks why we haven't called back, we can blame it on it.

Even if we don't own a machine, we call people who do. Don't we enjoy their **clever answering messages**, all those celebrity impersonations, witty conceits, charming little poems and songs, and dramatic monologues? No, we do not. They're tedious and embarrassing. And people who conduct their jobs out of their homes can never know who might be calling (and receiving a dreadful first impression). Rule Number One for owners of answering machines: No gimmicks. One couple, both professional musicians, recorded an answering message in dazzling eight-voice (overdubbed) harmony. It was a pleasure to hear, and to respond to. So let them be the exception. All others, play it straight.

In return, all callers should promise to include **the day and time of their call**. This courtesy, so frequently requested and so seldom granted, is especially useful when the callee has been out of town, and comes home to a string of messages left over the course of several days. Make it a habit of message-leaving: "Hi, this is [your name here], it's [day] at [time]," etc.

So you do. You leave your name, the day and time you've called, and ask Tom to call you back. The rest of the day passes without his return call, and you begin to wonder: **How long should I wait before I begin to feel a bit annoyed** at Tom?

Theoretically, at least, the crushing answer is: Forever. You cannot know where he is, if he has heard your message, even if he is alive. For practical purposes, though, give him two or three days, then try again.

Thus another paradox of the answering machine: that while it brings us as callers directly into the heart of a person's home, it nonetheless also provides a kind of absolute separation between him and us. We can hear his voice on the tape, and leave our message for as long as we wish. But as far as knowing where our callee is, and when we will hear from him, we may as well have gotten no answer at all.

Does that mean not having a machine is as good as having one? One source spoke of a friend who, although frequently on the road, has **no answering machine and subscribes to no answering service**. Is this, the source wondered, rude? Frustrating, yes; rude, no. (Unrealistic, definitely.) Outrageous as it may sound, a ringing telephone imposes no obligation on its owner to answer it, either in person or via mechanical or human surrogate. On the other hand, this source is perfectly entitled to be sick and tired of trying to reach this friend, and to decide it's not worth it, and to stop calling altogether.

A DISSENTING VIEW

How to respond to a telephone owner who refuses to take advantage of message-taking technology is mildly interesting. But let's reverse the perspective, and consider a more intriguing angle on the subject, from the point of view of the caller.

Suppose Jack has a friend named Judy, who **"hates answering machines." She refuses to talk to them.** On receiving the recorded answering message of Jack's machine, she hangs up in disgust. Is this, or is this not, bad form?

Let's add one assumption to sharpen the focus of this question: that the machine in use records the fact that someone has called whether or not the caller leaves a message. In such a case, Jack returns home to his machine, and discovers that the following took place: Someone called. The caller heard Jack's tape-recorded request that the caller identify himself. And the calller refused to do so, leaving instead a blank, blunt silence, or an annoying dial tone. This scenario suggests another quesiton: What is this, if *not* rude?

Not everyone agrees. One lady, an expert in etiquette who is rarely wrong about anything, in this case has stated that it is perfectly legitimate to hang up on an answering machine. When rebuked by a correspondent, who suggested that one would not, for example, hang up on a secretary or a footman, this lady—who is normally so acute about the effects of one's actions on others—has replied that the secretary and the footman have "feelings," but a machine does not.

Both of these statements are true. Still, this argument is nonsense. Jack, in fact, has feelings, and will be sensitive to rejection and discourtesy when he plays back the tape. The request that callers at least identify themselves is not the machine's, but its owner's. To pretend, as Judy does, that she is not hanging up on Jack, but only on "the machine," is is either extremely disingenuous, preposterously literal, or astoundingly primitive. The lady mentioned above would be appalled to learn that someone refused to respond to a wedding invitation's RSVP on the grounds that he "hated engraved paper" and "was ignoring the invitation, not the bride's family who sent it," adding, by way of explanation, that "invitations don't have feelings."

It is irrelevant whether or not inanimate objects "have feelings." What matters is that they are not moral agents. They therefore disappear in any discussion of morality, ethics, or etiquette, leaving the human beings on either side of them free to behave well or badly to one another, regardless of any technology that may be interposed between them for the purpose. You are not talking "to a machine." You are talking to a person *via* a machine.

It seems not to be asking too much, therefore, that you respect someone's desire to know who has called by leaving the most cursory of messages. That one of the machine owner's "feelings" is a desire to hear from you is made plain by the fact that he or she has provided the machine in the first place. Even if you don't take the provision of the machine as a courtesy to all callers—which, arguably, it is—you at least ought to take it as a request *for* a courtesy *from* all callers. That beep is the electronic age's way of saying, "The favor of a reply is requested." It is a discourtesy to ignore it.

Some machines "answer" with a **message that leaves the caller no clue as to whom he's reached**, announcing merely that the callee is not in, and asking the caller to leave a message. This is as deplorable as it is understandable. Certainly one doesn't wish to inform potential burglars who it is that is not home. Still, you should acknowledge that your caller has reached the right number by including a first name in the answering machine, or the complete phone number or, what is slightly cannier, just the last four digits of the phone number—something, at any rate, to assure most callers that they've reached the number they intended. The latter will even work when the caller is a stranger who has never spoken with you before and therefore could not be expected to recognize your unidentified voice.

As for **what else to feature on the answering message**, having stipulated above *not* to include celebrity impressions, dramatic intonations, original verse, music, etc., it only remains to add that some machines provide an unlimited length of time in which to leave a message, and some a set interval. Tell your callers which they have, so they know just how succinct they must be.

And **how should they leave a message?** In addition to the day and time, as begged for above, they should speak clearly, loudly, and slowly enough to be comprehensible. It's self-evident, yes, but many people take the machine's beep as a cue to perform; sometimes, amid the burst of creativity, you can't understand a word they've said. Endlessly rewinding and replaying cryptic, garbled messages may be vastly rewarding to spies and surveillance teams, but for the ordinary citizen it's a drag.

Leaving messages with an answering service is no different from leaving them with a secretary, although some services may be a bit too insistent that you leave something other than your name. They should not, and you needn't.

COMPUTER
*B*ULLETIN BOARDS

In General: **W**ith the proliferation of personal computers have come "computer bulletin boards," a new and very stylized way for people to meet, greet, talk, flirt, and offend one another. While specific rules of various services may vary, in general they work thus:

You sit at a computer, to which your telephone is hooked up via a modem. With communications software, you have the machine dial certain numbers, and in a moment you are linked up with a network of people from all over the country, reading their screens and typing their messages to one another. Everyone has a "handle," i.e., an assumed name, which can be changed at will. Their words appear on your screen, preceded by each person's handle. The dialogue will accomodate as many as wish to join it; smaller exchanges inevitably take shape, as two or more people converse mainly with each other as you sit, either eavesdropping (called "lurking") or "talking" with others.

If you wish to speak to someone privately, you may invite him or her, or several users, to "talk" or "chat." Entering the requisite commands sends all concerned onto a private channel. You may discuss whatever you want, however you wish, before returning to "open." Over time, people come and go, leave for a meal or an appointment, and return. Many regulars know one another, exchange news, ask about details in each other's lives, etc. (They may have long ago exchanged letters, phone calls, photos, or friendly embraces at parties or seminars.) Others, newcomers or infrequent users, make tentative contacts.

Meanwhile, you look up, and three hours have elapsed. You dread to think what this will look like on your phone bill. The next day or night, you can't wait to log on again.

Naturally there are rules of etiquette that apply to computer bulletin boards, many of which have to do with sex. Yes: sex. Via computer.

TYPE DIRTY TO ME, BABY

A lot of flirting takes place on the "open" channel of such bulletin boards—at least, it does on general interest ones—and it often leads to more graphic sexual exchanges when participants switch to a private channel. **Is that, in fact, the main purpose of the "talk" channels? Is an invitation to "chat" to be interpreted as a proposition?**

Not necessarily. Bear in mind that under normal conditions, your exchange with someone on "open" takes place amid several other conversations; your "Hi, there!" and his/her reply may be separated on the screen by five or ten lines of other people's messages. In order to stay in touch with your interlocutor, you must therefore watch the scrolling text carefully for his handle, which can be a strain on both the eyes and the patience. Slipping away to a private channel is often (in fact, usually) done simply for convenience. (An expert source estimates that about 75 percent of private conversations are nonsexual discussions of routine matters.)

Note, too, that usually by the time you have given or received an invitation to "talk," you have established a rapport with the other person on "open" that will set the tone of what ensues when you both agree to go private. Naturally, accepting such an invitation carries with it the implied awareness that more intimate matters could follow. But they are not to be taken for granted by either party.

MADAM, YOU'RE ADAM

Among the many slang expressions used for economy and effect on bulletin boards, one of the most ubiquitous is "MORF." It addresses a key fact which, in regular exchanges (in person, by telephone, and by CB radio) is usually one of the first to be disclosed but which, on bulletin boards, remains teasingly uncertain: Is the person you're talking to **Male OR Female?**

Interestingly, you can never really know, unless and until either you speak to the person on the phone or meet him/her in the flesh. Not only is a handle like ELEC-TRON opaque and ambiguous, but a seemingly more revealing one like SUZI Q is no guarantee that its owner is female. After all, there are almost certainly people who talk on such services precisely in order to masquerade as members of the opposite sex. If you want to know a person's gender, **is it rude to ask? Is it rude to refuse to answer? Is it rude to lie?**

This is even trickier than it seems. One of the central attractions of such networks is that participants encounter each other stripped of absolutely every characteristic that might lead them to prejudge, well or poorly, those with whom they speak. Hidden, until he or she wishes to disclose them, are the person's sex, race, appearance, age, height and weight, marital status, accent, level of education, wealth, clothes, profession—all those categories, in fact, about which *Mayflower Manners* obsesses twenty-four hours a day.

What remains—aside from the ability to speak English, and to type—is, in the words of one expert source, an encounter "soul to soul." Not that everyone you meet on these channels is particularly soulful; the range of humanity on computer bulletin boards is about the same as it is everywhere else. There are charmers, boors, wits, half-wits, etc. But you meet them as pure personalities, devoid of any physical qualities and free of all gender connotations. Not only is this their right, but it's what makes these bulletin boards the unique form of interactive communication they are.

On the other hand, you're entitled to want to know if the person with whom you are about to share a sexual fantasy is the sex you want him to be. Therefore, these rules:

1. It is rude to MORF on "open." It violates the spirit of the medium, and threatens to force someone to reveal his/her sex, not only to you (to whom the person may be willing to do so), but to everyone.

2. It is not rude to MORF in "talk." But . . .

3. It is not rude to refuse to answer a legitimately-asked MORF in "talk." Don't ignore it, or pretend you haven't "heard" it. Instead, simply decline politely to answer.

"But then I won't know if my partner is really a man or a woman," someone will object. To which the only response is: Exactly. You'll then have to decide whether or not to proceed. It's at moments like those that computer bulletin boards offer, not just technologically clever ways to communicate in place of being there in person, but unique experiences available no other way.

I COULDN'T HELP BUT OVERSEE YOUR CONVERSATION . . .

You're lurking, or you've just logged on, and you observe an exchange by two or three simpatico people. **Is it rude to try to join them,** to give greetings and then voice an opinion or ask a question concerning something they're discussing?

It's perfectly proper. "Open" is, after all, open, and the rules that govern its interactions should resemble those of a party: You loiter on the outskirts, you discreetly blend in, you take part, you don't dominate. If they resent your "intrusion," they are free to go to a private channel. Of course, you can't physically compel them to include you in their discussion, but at least you can introduce yourself and attempt to join in, secure in the knowledge that even while they ignore you and make you feel like an idiot, you have behaved properly. Isn't that at least a small consolation?

DO YOU COMMUNICATE INTERACTIVELY HERE OFTEN?

Sometimes it's possible to get the impression that people who talk frequently on bulletin boards do so precisely to avoid discussing personal issues such as jobs, family, money, etc. Their exchanges, for hours on end, can amount to little more than a frat-mixer come-on. That's all well and good, of course, but what if you find yourself in conversation with some other users, on "open," and are curious about just the mundane details of their lives? **Is it permissible to ask what they do for a living, where they live, their ages, etc.?** Or do even those kinds of inquiries violate the spirit of anonymity of the medium?

Not only is it permissible to ask, but you will probably get answers. On any given evening, the screen is dominated by several regulars who know as much as they want to about each other, and who have logged on to continue an epic flirtation that for all you know has been going on for years. Almost all the others, though, will be perfectly willing to share details of their lives. And even if not, you're entitled to ask.

YOU MEAN YOU'RE *NOT* THE KING OF SPAIN?

Finally, this possibly silly question: **Is it bad manners to lie?** After all, maybe the answer is no. With anonymity so integral a part of this form of communication, maybe telling untruths is all in the game. Is it?

No. Not only is it ethically wrong, it's bad manners, too. Good manners consist of not answering questions you don't want to answer by avoiding them gracefully. For example, a person not wanting to answer truthfully to a MORF might reply (as one source reports seeing), "MORF shield in place!" Not telling is all in the game. Lying is lying.

BIRTHS, ETC.

In General: In death we are all the same. It's birth that separates the men from the boys, the women from the girls, the boys from the girls, and the men from the women. The social revolution wrought by feminism over the past thirty years—let alone the past hundred—has had its effect on even this, the most unique and quintessential of female activities.

Not that men are now able to conceive, nurture, and deliver babies; such a development would be the most revolutionary in history, resulting in an overhaul (in America, at least) of every known social institution. This is because in America, women are considered by society to be "a special interest," while men are "society." Childbearing would therefore become a respected, rather than a romanticized, function, while child raising would be accorded the importance now reserved for achievements in business, athletics, and entertainment. Government itself would undergo a revision affecting just about every agency and institution with the exception of the already-appropriately-named Department of Labor.

Still, while men don't deliver babies, nor do they as commonly simply pace the waiting room, chain-smoking cigarettes and waiting to hand out cigars. For one thing, hospitals won't let them smoke. (Statistically, their wives are more likely to smoke than they, anyway.) The passive, anxiously useless Dad has more and more yielded to the actively participating Father, who in today's world finds himself part labor coach, part midwife, part staff photographer, part obstetrical assistant. Birth itself, to the previous generation a kind of glorified appendectomy (operating room, general anesthesia, passive mother, omnipotent surgeon) is as frequently today a kind of brief, intensive, do-it-mostly-yourself form of physical therapy (birthing suite, selective anesthesia, active mother, interactive obstetrician).

As for mothers, here's the paradox: in retaining more control and active participation in the process of delivery, they have made childbirth an occasion to display a female version of macho—"macha," as it were. And why not? Few achievements in art or athletics require as much concentrated discomfort, concentration, stamina, self-sacrifice, or fatigue. Conception is a pleasure, and happens in seconds; it's gestation and delivery that is the real accomplishment. Women therefore deserve to swagger a bit once they've been through it all, although of course by then they're lucky if they can get out of bed, let alone swagger. If they can, and have enough energy left over to take some pride in their performance, let them (within reason; see below). They probably know that their time for such glory is limited. In three or four years their creation will deposit melted chocolate on their new sofa, give them back talk when they rebuke him, and then complain that he likes Daddy better.

LAMAZE, LES MAS, LES PAS, ETC.

Did our mothers and fathers take **"classes" in giving birth?** No—but look how we turned out. No wonder so many parents-to-be feel the need to do so. Why start making irrevocable mistakes in child rearing before you absolutely have to?

Such classes offer several unusual opportunities, not only for men to witness the relatively rare spectacle of a dozen pregnant women together in one room, but for women to broach subjects that under other circumstances might seem a bit more taboo. For example, while most women attend Lamaze classes with their husbands— well, with a man, who we may assume is both the woman's husband and the father of her baby—some can be seen with others: an older woman (probably her mother), a friend, etc. (One source told of a class where the mother-to-be attended with her own mother, for the reason— which she volunteered—that her husband refused, on grounds of squeamishness, to take part in the delivery.) One might be tempted to **inquire as to the whereabouts of the father**. But one should not. Asking, "Where's your husband?" at a dinner party is one thing, but at a birth class implies disapproval. Even if asked in the most warm, supportive, and caring way possible, it's essentially nobody else's business.

Despite everyone's firm intentions to learn the techniques and do the breathing with discipline and concentration, the question that haunts Lamaze classes is: will you use drugs? (Thus do women encounter the two-edged sword of macho, and discover that the privilege of strutting around displaying one's strength is always accompanied by the temptation, with its implicit disgrace, to take the easier way out.) Even when the instructor's not listening, **is it legitimate to ask fellow students about their intentions to use epidurals, other anesthetics, etc.?** Or is it like leaning over to a neighbor at a meeting of Alcoholics Anonymous and asking if, after the meeting, he'd like to go out for a beer?

The answer depends on context. If the subject comes up and is rendered legitimate by enough rueful laughs and unsolicited confessions, there's nothing traitorous or backsliding about asking and answering. If, however, everyone around you is putting on a brave face while you have an urge to ask the unaskable, don't do it. You may think your sister mothers are living in a dream world— or you may wish to recruit sympathy for your own fears —but it would be unsporting to insist on a discussion which all have agreed, by their presence at the class, they wish (at least to try) to circumvent.

Outside the Lamaze class the rule is a bit more stringent. One common complaint of pregnant women is that the world seems to regard them as its ward, subjecting them to unsolicited advice and intrusive questions and even, sometimes, unsolicited tummy-pats, simply because they are with child. The world, for its part, should remember that while children are indeed a responsibility of all people, women bearing children are sovereign adults, entitled to as much privacy and consideration as any nonpregnant man. Other etiquette authorities have written eloquently about the unacceptability of addressing pregnant women with "Hey, big mama!" or placing your hand on the swelling tummy of a woman not your spouse as though appreciating the heft of a competitive pumpkin at the County Fair, or asking all sorts of nosy questions from "How much weight have you gained?" to "Do you want a boy or a girl?"

Omitted, thus far, has been a discussion of more sophisticated, but no less intrusive, banter. Men (or women) hip to contemporary childbearing should nonetheless refrain from asking, "Are you doing Lamaze?" and/or "Are you using drugs?" Naturally, such talk is fine between friends, although even friends should be aware of the insensitive nature of the topic, and tread lightly. Acquaintances, colleagues, and strangers should treat such matters as they would any other medical state of affairs. Asking how a pregnant woman feels is a kindness, provided asking does not become prying, and polite interest become expert, or pseudo-expert, lecturing. Inquiring about how the woman intends to conduct her childbirth—preparatory to approving of her philosophy or not—is rude.

WHAT DO YOU SAY TO A PREGNANT LADY?

Even if you're not particularly interested in the technicalities of a childbirth, there are always other things to be curious about. And men, these days, might think it especially sharp or knowing or up-to-date to ask about them. Say a friend of yours, who is over a certain age, has announced that she's pregnant. Is it okay if you knowledgeably **ask if she intends to have amniocentesis or CVS?**

Alas, no. She, and those in earshot, may be suitably impressed that you, as a dunderhead male, know about such things. But they remain entirely her business, to be discussed only with the father, her physician, her health insurance company, and any journalists or sociologists who may be doing relevant studies. Do not, therefore, inquire as to how the tests turned out. And it goes without saying—well, it goes with saying, since we're taking the trouble to say it here—that if you somehow learn that **the results of such tests are less than**

optimal, you may not ask, no matter how sympathetically, "What are you going to do?" It is hard to conceive of a subject more personal.

This holds for women as well as men, and the answer is the same if you happen to know that the woman has recently been **tested for pregnancy itself.** And to those readers who find themselves thinking that *of course* one doesn't pry into such matters, and *of course* all aspects of pregnancy are highly personal and to be discussed only at the discretion of the woman in question, this reply: Of course of course. But if all people were as sensible and sensitive as you, there would be no need for the etiquette industry, and the vast subject of manners would shrink to a series of token reminders about how to eat a lobster in public and write a thank-you letter to the Pope.

But now the woman in question declares to one and all with untrammeled joy that she is with child, and all tests are negative, all coasts are clear for a happy pregnancy and a healthy child. Life is bliss, but as an onlooker or, better, a close friend, you happen to know: she is not married. So what? Times have changed. Fine. But say she is neither "living with," "seeing," "dating steadily," "going with," or in any other way regularly having sex with the same identifiable man. The question arises in one's scrupulously well-mannered mind: **Who is the father?** Dare one ask?

Absolutely not.

Even if you have not seen this woman for nine months, and at your next encounter she sports an infant on her hip, stifle the question. You need not stifle oblique allusions and loaded queries meant to prompt her to volunteer the information, but for God's sake be tactful, and err on the side of ignoring the whole thing. If you are a friend, you probably know. If you are a friend and don't know, there may be an important reason why not, one being that the mother herself isn't sure. If you are not a friend, and more a colleague or an acquaintance, asking the identity of the child's father is equivalent to the mother asking you whom you slept with nine months ago.

THE PARTUM'S OVER

You've had the baby. Say the experience was painful and exhausting and overwhelming enough to provide you with a real sense of accomplishment afterward, a sense that you've earned your stripes as a mother and a woman. Naturally, following a suitable period of rest and retreat with the new infant, when you once again greet friends, you will want to brag. Among the women who are themselves mothers, you'll want your experience validated, your membership in the club approved. Among other women, you may (if the subject comes up) find yourself hinting at the profundity of the experience. Fine.

But don't, unless you're in the exclusive company of women discussing only this subject, **talk about your delivery in explicit detail**. There may be people present less enthralled with the specifics than you. (One of them may be your husband.) In fact—and this will have no bearing on how they regard your child—they may be disgusted. Besides, no one besides another mother will respond with sufficient admiration or commiseration.

If your audience includes confirmed nonparents, most will respond in one of three ways: with barely-veiled disinterest, barely-gratifying polite interest, or barely-adequate real interest. Part of the dissatisfaction you will feel will be an inevitable consequence, not of your audience, but your own intensity of experience. GIs who have seen battle come back with only so much tolerance for the opinions of those who haven't.

And besides, one can never be sure whether nonparents today have attained that state willingly or with great reluctance, nor whether they remain in it sadly, defensively, proudly, or (after they hear your tale) with relief. Having children, formerly a pursuit taken for granted by most of middle-class society, has become much more problematic for reasons amply documented each month in several hundred women's magazines: careers, later ages of marriage, "the man shortage," divorce, etc. People are self-conscious about it as never before. And into this charged atmosphere comes glowing, tired, triumphant you, ready to gab about your episiotomy? Resist the impulse. Childbearing is a central human experience, and birth an awe-inspiring miracle, and so forth, but leave the gory details to chats with your doctor, other mothers, and your husband if he seems willing to listen.

The need for this advice is particularly urgent among women who have, for whatever reason, **delivered in unorthodox circumstances**: at home on the sofa, in the car, etc. The novelty (and relief) of having a baby in a cab—delivered by a daddy, cabbie, or cop—is appreciable, and everyone will want to hear the logistical plot-points and laugh ruefully at your predicament. Be aware, though, that to your listeners it's Feydeau, not Obstetrics 101.

This stricture holds for the birth announcement, an optional notification of the newborn's arrival that should be succinct, muted, and, if it must be cute, never cutesy.

You may want to tell the world that you went all-natural, with no drugs, no anesthesia, no hospital, no doctor—only a midwife, a pot of boiling water, a penknife, and a bottle of Jim Beam. But keep all that off the announcement, encapsulating it into, perhaps, this:

Mr. and Mrs. Goodman Parent Joyfully Announce
the Birth of
A Son
Boy Fairchild
Born at Home, 30 February, 1990
(optional: weight and length)

The point is, while people engage in unusual birthing practices for a number of perfectly valid, and even praiseworthy, philosophical, political, and religious reasons, such reasons do not justify foisting the surgical details on innocent bystanders, regardless of how exultant the mother and sublime the event.

And to those **new mothers challenged by seasoned veterans to compare ordeals** (dosages of Pitocin, numbers of epidurals, conscientiousness of obstetrician, etc.), this: You may decline to take part with a cheery, weary, "Oh, I don't even want to think about all that now. I'm just glad he/she is finally here," etc.

PICTURES AND AN EXHIBITION

Then there are the **photographs.** Pass them around with delicacy and tact, applying the same caution as discussed above. The point is to show your babe at his or her time of maximum innocence, not to thrust pictures of a recent medical procedure in people's faces.

As for **videotapes** of the birth itself, you are saved from much possible harm by the fact that such tapes need VCRs and televisions in order to be seen. You can't, that is to say, whip them out at a friend's luncheon and compel all present to watch. if you are visited at home, and you do not wish your friends or relatives to share vicariously in the experience, don't say, "Hey, let's watch the tape of Scott-Max's birth!" Instead, delicately allow as how "we taped his birth," and pause, smiling slightly, communicating a fetching amusement at the well-known but understandable folly, common to doting parents the world over, of presuming that others are as interested in the details of their child's birth as they. Then wait for the gang to call for the tape. They probably won't; they showed up to celebrate your victorious return from travail, not to watch you go through it all over again. But if they do, you've pulled it off nicely.

Suppose, though, as a friend of the parents who would rather not avail yourself of visual aids regarding the birth, you are nonetheless handed the pix. Well, that's easy: a quick glance, a murmured, "What a lovely baby," and pass them on. And if your host or hostess urges you to savor all sixty-four photos, and provides a running commentary on the nurse, the obstetrician, the food at the hospital, etc. just hand them on with another comment about the baby. (When in doubt, praise the newborn. That's all the parents really want to hear anyway.)

But now you discover that the momentum of the party has deposited you before the TV to witness footage of Scott-Max's birth, in living color and stereophonic sound. And you'd rather not. What do you say? **How do you get out of watching the tape?**

Rise, excuse yourself as though going to the bathroom, and go to the bathroom. Have a glass of water, wash your face, whistle "Dixie"—anything to occupy a minute or so. And then look for something or someone distracting in the kitchen. If no one is there, try asking your host if you may make a quick phone call. Do that, preferably from a phone as far from the proceedings as possible, more preferably to someone who will indulge, with a lengthy and untaxing chat, your need to avoid looking at the TV until the show is over. Or loiter near a bookshelf and browse. Strive to remember that after all, you are within your rights. Scott-Max is the most important fact of his parents' lives, and you are in their home . . . but his arrival is not strictly your concern.

On the contrary: You're a guest, and entitled to all the privileges appertaining thereto.

BABY, IT'S YOU

Of course, some parents are not content merely to hand around photos of the baby. Some (usually people for whom this is not the first child) offer to hand around the baby itself. Many people find this very disconcerting, fearing that they'll drop, fumble, or otherwise mishandle the infant and precipitate disaster. There are others who, though confident about their ability to hold a seven-pound creature without breaking it, nonetheless "don't like" babies. One can see why. Babies are unpredictable. They may excrete unpleasant substances without warning, burst into noisy squalls for no apparent reason, and ignore all entreaties to pipe down. The only way to charm them is to behave in an undignified manner. All of one's ready store of wit, learning, and sophistication are useless, because babies *just don't care* about all that. When Mom offers up the bundled babe and asks if you'd like to hold her, **is there a polite way to decline?**

Fortunately, yes. The trick (as always) is to deflect the offer by complimenting the parent or rejoicing in the child. See chart, following.

HOW TO AVOID HOLDING THE BABY

What the Baby Is Doing When Mother Offers Her	What You Say, After "Oh, No, Thank You"
Sleeping soundly	"I don't want to wake her."
Looking around quietly	"I love to see the two of you together."
Laughing, giggling, etc.	"She's so delighted to be with you."
Pouting, "crabbing"	"One look at me and she'll burst into tears."
Crying	"You're so good with her."

The existence of a new baby is sometimes only marginally more exciting than the various **unusual methods of gestation** that may have attended its creation. Science has discovered a number of ways of compensating for Nature's shortcomings, including in vitro fertilization, sperm bank donations, surrogate mothering, fertility-enhancing drugs, etc. Intimates of the parents might, now that the baby is a reality, feel a bit more tempted to ask various questions they've been harboring for months but have been reluctant to press on the expectant mother. Is the baby's (or, in the case of fertility drugs, babies') arrival a signal to indulge their curiosity?

Not directly, no. Once again, the relatively public fact of a newborn is one thing, the essentially private nature of its creation another. Close friends will probably have been given signals all along as to what aspect of the experience the parents will and will not discuss; those given no signals should assume that the subject is not up for discussion. Friends, relatives, and colleagues should likewise take their cue from the parents, and assume that if a certain topic is not raised by Mom or Dad (such as the feelings of Mom about having the egg fertilized in a lab, or the actual identity of Dad), then it should not be raised by anyone else, either.

Even when **fertility drugs** have been used and acknowledged, resulting in the relatively rare and spectacular appearance of two, three, or more babies, conversation should be about the kids, and not the drugs. (And, of course, the status of the mother.) Besides, all unasked questions in such cases probably come down to one central rhetorical question anyway, viz., "Boy, you really got more than you bargained for, didn't you?" Such an observation is not only presumptuous (the parents may have got exactly what they bargained for), but it pales before the immediate joy, and gigantic responsibility, facing the parents. The correct thing to do in such circumstances is to be helpful, not smart.

Book Mark

The text of this book was set in the typeface Caslon 540 and the display was set in Caslon Extra Condensed with Swash by Crane Typesetting Service, Inc., West Barnstable, Massachusetts.

It was printed on 50 lb. Glatfelter, an acid-free paper, and bound by RR Donnelley, Harrisonburg, Virginia.

DESIGNED BY
DIANE STEVENSON/SNAP · HAUS GRAPHICS